LONG BEACH STATE *at* 75

LONG BEACH STATE *at* 75

BARBARA KINGSLEY-WILSON

GREENLEAF
BOOK GROUP PRESS

Published by Greenleaf Book Group Press
Austin, Texas
www.gbgpress.com

Distributed by Greenleaf Book Group

For ordering information or special discounts for bulk purchases, please contact Greenleaf Book Group at PO Box 91869, Austin, TX 78709, 512.891.6100.

Design and composition by Greenleaf Book Group
Cover design by Greenleaf Book Group
Please see Photo Credits page for copyright information
for all photos other than the following:
Grads from 2021 gather at the Go Beach! letters for the
traditional photo. Photo by Richard H. Grant;
Students from the early 1960s move in between classes at the new Liberal Arts 1
building. Photo from the University Archives;
Students pose by a billboard for the new campus in the 1950s.
Photo from the University Archives.

Publisher's Cataloging-in-Publication data is available.

Print ISBN: 979-8-88645-222-8

eBook ISBN: 979-8-88645-223-5

To offset the number of trees consumed in the printing of our books, Greenleaf donates a portion of the proceeds from each printing to the Arbor Day Foundation. Greenleaf Book Group has replaced over 50,000 trees since 2007.

Printed in Canada on acid-free paper

24 25 26 27 28 29 30 31 10 9 8 7 6 5 4 3 2 1

First Edition

PREFACE

If I could request a superpower, it would not be flying, or the option to become invisible at will; it would be time travel.

I would love to see what people were thinking, saying, and doing in times past. One of my first stops would be late 1940s Long Beach, when students stepped over construction debris in newly converted mid-century apartments at a new "college" with a ridiculously long name—Los Angeles–Orange County State College.

This interest led me to write *Long Beach State: A Brief History* in 2015. When I got the chance to do another book, this time a coffee table photo book for the university's seventy-fifth anniversary, I thought, *Why not?*

I've listened to recordings, perused archives, and talked to former students, faculty, and administrators to find out how California State University, Long Beach, known historically and informally as Long Beach State, got its improbable start and continued to grow to become a major university.

As any alum or employee will tell you, there's *so* much that goes into a university: students, academics, social life, sports, campus protests, friendships, and assorted drama.

This book is like a survey course, and highlights some of the foundational events, people, and experiences that have made Long Beach State unique.This includes the sacred Native American land on which the college was built.

This "through the decades" look at the college's history is reminiscent of email threads. For example, library director Charles Boorkman got his start with the college in 1949 (making him a great history resource). His story is listed in the 1950s, since that's when he started getting the resources to build the collection and facility that helped make the library what it is today.

This book tells the story through faculty, administrators, and students. For some, we hear from them in their own words. I talked to people who helped the university grow and grew themselves while spending their formative years going to class on upper campus, wrestling with parking, cheering at basketball games in the Goldmine or during volleyball games in the Walter Pyramid.

In addition to the stories gathered through interviews, much information came from Special Collections at the University Library. (Thank you, archivist Heather Steele, for your patient assistance!) Long Beach State Athletics were also a huge help as were the folks at Strategic Communications, especially photographer Sean DuFrene. *The Daily Forty-Niner* and campus yearbook archives were enormously useful as well, along with the Historical Society of Long Beach. Thanks also to longtime facilities chief Jon Regnier and countless others who patiently offered their time and perspective. Thanks, also to my family for putting up with my repeated requests to review copy or just ideas as I put together this book.

This coffee table book certainly doesn't capture all the events, majors, and colleges of the past seventy-five years, but attempts to give a flavor of what it was like, how this campus has changed, and how students were influenced by their individual journeys at Long Beach State.

BARBARA KINGSLEY-WILSON
December 2023

1940s and 1950s

Instruction began on September 28, 1949, with 169 students, who registered for classes at a fruit stand on Pacific Coast Highway. The college that would become Long Beach State grew out of Fred Bixby's old alfalfa and bean fields and launched its first classes in a partially developed apartment complex on Anaheim Road.

The college set up shop in the present-day Park Estates neighborhood, and parking even then was scarce; students were encouraged to carpool. The first students stepped over concrete and rebar to get to class. Desks and chairs were prison-issue, and there were no library books to be found. The first faculty meeting was held outdoors under a California pepper tree. No one, not even the biggest college boosters then, could have predicted that Long Beach State would grow to become one of the most applied-to universities in the nation.

"Site of the Proposed Long Beach State College," as it was photographed in 1947, while still part of the Bixby Ranch.

1940s

THERE'S NO COMPELLING REASON WHY LONG BEACH GOT A COLLEGE WHEN IT DID IN 1949.

Yes, the area was growing dramatically after World War II, but so were Orange County, Lakewood, and lots of other communities, as farmland was being plowed under for single-family homes and apartments at a breakneck pace.

Indeed, Downey was lobbying hard for a new college, as were cities in Orange County—which went as far as creating a pamphlet picturing a smog-choked LA County next to a green, wide-open O. C. The college founders even gave the college the ungainly temporary name of Los Angeles–Orange County State College, so as not to offend any of the factions jockeying for a new institution of higher learning.

LINCOLN
J. G. RANDALL

STREET FINAL

LONG BEACH INDEPENDENT

Long Beach 12, Calif., Tuesday Morning, March 22, 1949

5 Cents

LONG BEACH TO GET FOUR-YEAR COLLEGE

Committees Picked by GOP Here

Ask Police Protect No. 4 Repeal Aides

Long Beach Independent

Extra Pay for Assemblymen

Alamitos Heights 1st Choice

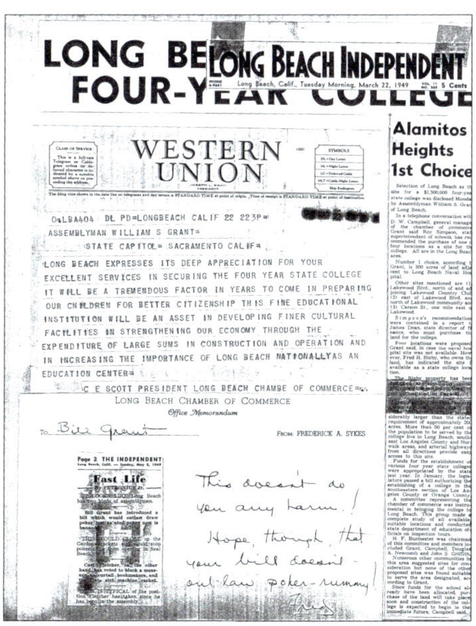
LONG BEACH INDEPENDENT

Long Beach, Calif., Tuesday Morning, March 22, 1949

5 Cents

WESTERN UNION

O LBA404 DL PD=LONGBEACH CALIF 22 223P=

ASSEMBLYMAN WILLIAM S GRANT=

STATE CAPITOL= SACRAMENTO CALIF=

LONG BEACH EXPRESSES ITS DEEP APPRECIATION FOR YOUR EXCELLENT SERVICES IN SECURING THE FOUR YEAR STATE COLLEGE IT WILL BE A TREMENDOUS FACTOR IN YEARS TO COME IN PREPARING OUR CHILDREN FOR BETTER CITIZENSHIP THIS FINE EDUCATIONAL INSTITUTION WILL BE AN ASSET IN DEVELOPING FINER CULTURAL FACILITIES IN STRENGTHENING OUR ECONOMY THROUGH THE EXPENDITURE OF LARGE SUMS IN CONSTRUCTION AND OPERATION AND IN INCREASING THE IMPORTANCE OF LONG BEACH NATIONALLYAS AN EDUCATION CENTER=

C E SCOTT PRESIDENT LONG BEACH CHAMBE OF COMMERCE=

LONG BEACH CHAMBER OF COMMERCE

Office Memorandum

To Bill Grant

From FREDERICK A. SYKES

Page 2 THE INDEPENDENT

Fast Life

This doesn't do you any harm! Hope, though, that your bill doesn't out-law poker-rummy! Fred

Alamitos Heights 1st Choice

THE HUMAN SPIRIT AND A GOLDEN DREAM

REMARKS BY PROFESSOR IRVING AHLQUIST

on August 27, 1999, at the College of Liberal Arts fiftieth anniversary luncheon

The two decades following World War II may be nostalgically seen as the Golden Age of the College Student. While campus populations swelled in numbers with the discharge of veterans armed with benefits from the G.I. Bill, the democratization of higher education became a hallmark of the era.

For me, also a veteran, who had been stationed in California for a brief period of time, there was the realization that California had stolen my heart and beckoned me to become a twentieth-century forty-niner, minus the Golden Fleece. Having finished all my doctoral work but my dissertation before my service in the army, I completed my thesis and earned my PhD at the University of Illinois in 1947. I immediately accepted a position at Northern Iowa University, then known as Iowa State Teachers College.

Two years later I met Dr. P. Victor Peterson, who had just been recruited by the California Legislature to establish a new college in southeastern Los Angeles County or Orange County. Within days Dr. Peterson offered me a position at $4,200 a year in yet-to-be-built Los Angeles-Orange County State College, whose permanent location had not been determined. Here was a golden opportunity to be a part of a new college, free of crippling traditions and open to new ideas and programs.

With no street address and no campus buildings, my wife, three-year-old son, and I arrived in Long Beach after a long drive cross-country. I drove too far south on PCH and ended up in Seal Beach. I asked several citizens about the location of a new college, with no one able to answer my question. Eventually, I was given an answer that led me to Park Estates, off PCH and Anaheim Street—and all I found were piles of lumber and some skeletal frames for apartment buildings that would ultimately be designated as the temporary site of the new college.

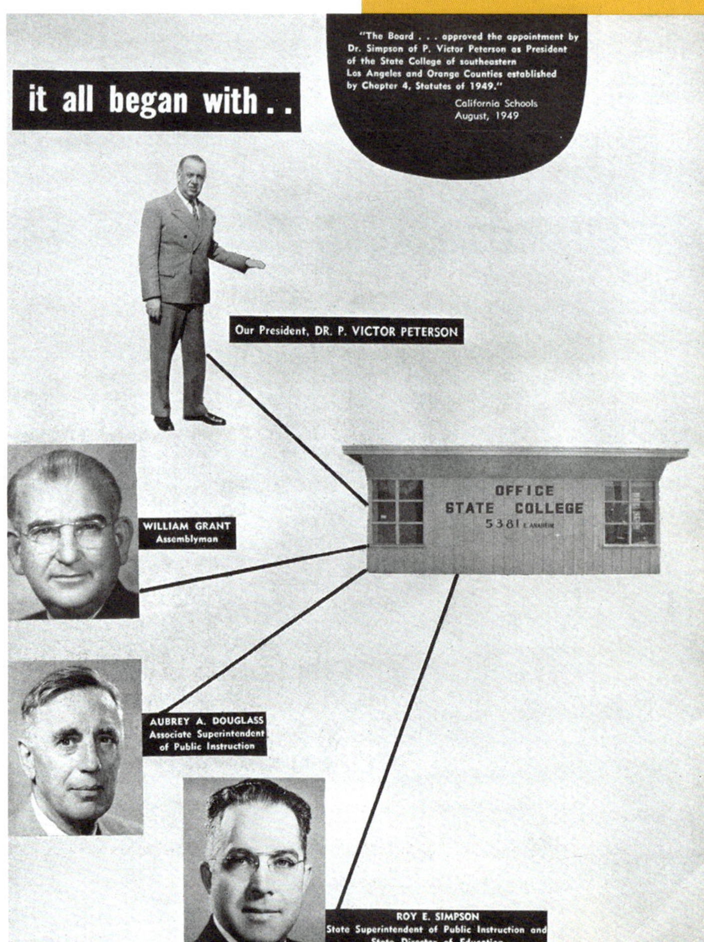

Within a few days, other faculty members joined me—thirteen of us in all—and our first faculty meeting was held under some pepper trees at 6201 Anaheim Road, with no street address yet posted. These first faculty members had earned doctorates from Yale, Michigan, Minnesota, Illinois, Wisconsin, Rome, Stanford, UCLA, and USC. Though education courses dominated the curricula, the liberal arts were represented in eight disciplines, all upper division classes: English, economics, geography, history, psychology, political science, sociology, and speech. For the students, 169 in all, that first semester gave them significant choices from forty-one classes.

We were a close-knit faculty, with an interdisciplinary orientation and a spirit of cooperation, whether called upon to move prison-made furniture for classes and offices, help with handling books for a nonexistent library, or participate in social activities, many of which were initiated by students, all of whom were between the ages of twenty and mid-forties. A big percentage were veterans whose education had been interrupted by the war and housewives who had married and had families.

Here were the students of '49, all of whom presented a challenge to us faculty members—with a few of us younger than they. To this day, they form a part of our memories and continue to be a part of us by correspondence, Ma Bell, email, and fax machines. To all of them, I shall ever be grateful for giving to me, now an octogenarian, a rich and meaningful postdoctoral education not found in historical archives or books but in the demonstrations of the meaning of the human spirit. To them and succeeding generations of students, I owe a great debt: They gave me the privilege of sharing with them my knowledge of the past and encouraging me in my pursuit of a golden dream, which has survived the passage of time.

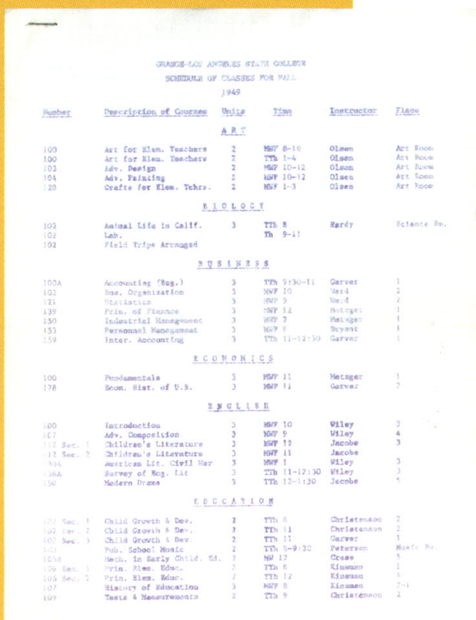

ORANGE-LOS ANGELES STATE COLLEGE
SCHEDULE OF CLASSES FOR FALL
1949

Number	Description of Courses	Units	Time	Instructor	Place
	ART				
100	Art for Elem. Teachers	2	MWF 8-10	Olsen	Art Room
100	Art for Elem. Teachers	2	TTh 1-4	Olsen	Art Room
103	Adv. Design	2	MWF 10-12	Olsen	Art Room
104	Adv. Painting	2	MWF 10-12	Olsen	Art Room
120	Crafts for Elem. Tchrs.	2	MWF 1-3	Olsen	Art Room
	BIOLOGY				
102	Animal Life in Calif.	3	TTh 8	Hardy	Science Rm.
102	Lab.		Th 9-11		
102	Field Trips Arranged				
	BUSINESS				
100A	Accounting (Beg.)	3	TTh 9:30-11	Garver	1
102	Bus. Organization	3	MWF 10	Ward	2
121	Statistics	3	MWF 9	Ward	2
139	Prin. of Finance	3	MWF 12	Metzger	1
150	Industrial Management	3	MWF 7	Metzger	1
153	Personnel Management	3	MWF 9	Bryant	1
159	Inter. Accounting	3	TTh 11-12:30	Garver	1
	ECONOMICS				
100	Fundamentals	3	MWF 11	Metzger	1
178	Econ. Hist. of U.S.	3	MWF 11	Garver	2
	ENGLISH				
100	Introduction	3	MWF 10	Wiley	3
107	Adv. Composition	3	MWF 9	Wiley	4
112 Sec. 1	Children's Literature	3	MWF 12	Jacobs	3
112 Sec. 2	Children's Literature	3	MWF 11	Jacobs	
130A	American Lit. Civil War	3	MWF 1	Wiley	3
136A	Survey of Eng. Lit	3	TTh 11-12:30	Wiley	3
150	Modern Drama	3	TTh 12-1:30	Jacobs	5
	EDUCATION				
102 Sec. 1	Child Growth & Dev.	2	TTh 8	Christensen	2
102 Sec. 2	Child Growth & Dev.	2	TTh 11	Christensen	2
102 Sec. 3	Child Growth & Dev.	2	TTh 11	Garver	1
103	Pub. School Music	2	TTh 8-9:30	Peterson	Music Rm.
105B	Mech. in Early Child. Ed.	2	MW 12	Cross	5
106 Sec. 1	Prin. Elem. Educ.	2	TTh 8	Kinsman	1
106 Sec. 2	Prin. Elem. Educ.	2	TTh 12	Kinsman	4
107	History of Education	3	MWF 8	Kinsman	2-1
109	Tests & Measurements	2	TTh 9	Christensen	2

The very first schedule of classes from 1949 and college beginnings laid out in the 1950 Prospector yearbook (left).

"YOU HAD THE SENSE YOU WERE STARTING SOMETHING"

Long Beach State's September 28, 1949, opening was postponed by repeated construction delays.

"Gestalt theory was filtered through the sounds of jackhammer and SKIL saw," said one account published in the first yearbook. Electricians, plumbers, and painters seemed to outnumber students, who stepped over lumber, paint buckets, and tarpaulins on their way to both registration and class. To get away from construction noise, one English professor led his class to the edge of the college dump. Students sat on pieces of cardboard. It was crude, but it was quiet.

A chronic shortage of typewriters and office equipment at the new school meant delays in ordering textbooks. According to a history penned by Charles Boorkman, the first librarian, the book budget was "lost in the bureaucratic mill in Sacramento" until November, when the first book purchase was approved, according to an unpublished history of the college. The temporary library was completed by November 10, but the first book didn't arrive until December 6. A makeshift canteen fashioned from a converted washroom served what were described as "Miller sandwiches" by World War II vets—two dry pieces of bread and a thin slice of ham or some other meat wrapped in paper and sold for fifteen cents.

But those first students remarked at what a friendly, close place the new college was. The professors were roughly the same age as the students, many of whom were returning from war service.

(Opposite page) The Civic League of Long Beach urged voters to approve $1 million in oil revenues for the new college. They did, by a 10-1 margin.

CIVIC LEAGUE OF LONG BEACH
410 Kress Bldg.
Long Beach 12, Calif.

R E S O L U T I O N

WHEREAS The California State Public Works Commission has announced a decision to build a new four-year State College in Long Beach for approximately 5000 students; and

WHEREAS this decision is announced is contingent upon the donation of a suitable site to the State by the City; and

WHEREAS a suitable site has been approved which can be purchased for approximately $1,000,000.00, and that funds for such purchase will be available from Upland Oil Revenues; and

WHEREAS the financial returns to the community will be many times the investment in the site both from the original construction and the subsequent operation and administration costs, and from increased housing and student activities; and

WHEREAS the cultural benefits and educational advantages accruing to Long Beach and the surrounding community from the existance of such an institution will far outweigh this initial investment in the required land;

BE IT THEREFORE RESOLVED:

That the Civic League of Long Beach, by unanimous action of its Board of Directors, hereby urges the approval by the voters of the ballot measure in the election of June 6th, 1950 which authorizes the City Council of Long Beach to purchase this land and donate it to the State of California as the site for constructing and operating said four-year College.

* * * *

Members of the Civic League:

The above Resolution was presented to the City Council of Long Beach on April 18, 1950. Publicity in local papers carried this story.

You have undoubtedly read about this proposed Charter Amendment and studied its provisions. Please indicate your approval or disapproval of the Ballot Issue on the enclosed form, and return at once to the office of the CIVIC LEAGUE, 410 Kress Bldg., Long Beach 12, Calif.

☑ yes

☐ No E. Clayton Burgess

They drank coffee and ate together in the canteen. "You had the sense you were starting something," said Isabel Patterson, one of the first students.

In June 1950, Long Beach residents voted overwhelmingly to use oil money to purchase just over 300 acres of hilly land from Fred Bixby. The college was quickly named Long Beach State College.

Students would use the apartments for two more years, running classes seven days a week until ten at night, before moving into temporary quarters on the new campus and then into permanent buildings starting in 1953. The buildings were few, and the new college land seemed vast, at least in the mid-1950s.

Boyd Davis, an industrial education professor when the campus opened, recalled his first trip to see the new campus set on a sloping hill off Seventh Street in East Long Beach.

"There was nothing there but a dog, a shepherd, and a flock of sheep," Boyd told the *Daily Forty-Niner* (which was originally known as the *Forty-Niner*) years later. "At the time a lot of people thought, 'why do we need all that land?' Many wanted to sell some of it."

(Opposite page) Builder Lloyd Whaley envisioned the new college as a centerpiece of his post-war development of booming east Long Beach.

President P. Victor Peterson addresses the first class of students in 1949.

THE MALIBU plan 4-B
now – come and see the
complete community – LOS ALTOS
Everything you need for complete living
is already here parks, schools, churches,
industry, a multi-million dollar shopping center
all part of a community plan developed over
10 years, and protected by the Los Altos Association
of 6000 families. AND you're within blocks
of the new $25,000,000 Long Beach State College.
AND LOS ALTOS biggest growth is coming
in 1954, with the growth of the new $25,000,000
Long Beach State College, just a few
blocks from your new home!
see FURNISHED EXHIBIT HOMES
in the 17th Unit
SALES OFFICES 2800 Bellflower Blvd.
2703 Palo Verde Ave.
FURNISHED EXHIBIT HOMES
in the 18th Unit
SALES OFFICES Studebaker Rd. and Atherton St.
Studebaker Rd. and Anaheim St.
by Aaron Schultz OPEN EVERY DAY 9 a.m. to 8 p.m.
Firestone Blvd.
Santa Ana Freeway
Spring St.
Lakewood Blvd.
Bellflower Blvd.
17
Studebaker
Stearns St.
Shopping Center
Atherton St.
Pacific Coast Hwy.
Palo Verde Ave.
18
State College
Anaheim St.
7th St.
Vet. Hosp.
Garden Grove Blvd.

TIMELINE:

THE FIRST YEAR

(Opposite page) Dean of administration David Bryant addresses students as classes begin.

January 27, 1949. Governor Earl Warren signs Assembly Bill No. 8, Ch. 4, which provides for the establishment of the college. UC Regents and State Board of Education survey recommended establishment of a state college to serve Orange and southeast Los Angeles counties.

Spring 1949. A state college division committee and P. Victor Peterson convince local developer Lloyd Whaley to stall completion of apartment buildings on Anaheim Road in the future Park Estates so college classrooms could be built there.

September 16. Santa Ana offers the Santa Ana City College site for the new college. Other offers include the Sunny Hills area in Fullerton and the Bixby Estate in Long Beach.

September 26–27. Despite the uncertainty, registration begins for fall semester, drawing 160 students: ninety-one female and sixty-nine male. (Nine students would be added later.) Cost of enrollment for full-time students is $17.50, with a $5 ASB fee included.

September 28. Instruction begins, morning classes only. All classes are upper division.

November 2. First student council meeting. Roger Bryson is chosen president.

October 27. Peterson hosts a dinner in the Long Beach Masonic Temple for the faculty and their spouses.

November 11. The *Forty-Niner* publishes its first issue on four mimeographed sheets. The office is a tool shed with a leaky roof.

April 5, 1950. State Public Works Commission votes to approve Long Beach site, on the condition that the site be annexed by the city and donated to the state.

June 6, 1950. Long Beach voters approve the appropriation of 320 acres of land for the establishment of the college. The next day, state director of education, Roy Simpson, names the campus Long Beach State College.

June 16, 1950. First commencement held at Hughes Junior High School. In a speech to the thirty-one graduates, Aubrey Douglass, director of the State College Division of the Department of Education, predicts that there will be 500 students at the college by 1958.

(Opposite page) A washroom was converted into a campus canteen for students and faculty in 1949.

"We drove down the coast, coming to Long Beach on that September day, early September . . . looking for what was going to be a college. I missed it. The directions were given. It was obvious why I missed it . . . ended up in Seal Beach, and all I got was a sulfur odor. We found the site in Park Estates, with just nothing but stacks of lumber. The reality of the situation was such that it suddenly hit me face on: No buildings. No library. Nothing."

—IRVING AHLQUIST, history professor and one of the founding faculty at Long Beach State

"When I went from Long Beach City College, I went downtown. Someone mentioned it . . . They gave me the name and I went to this man's office. And I told him who I was, and I said, 'Now, I'm going to, I plan to go to (U)SC. But I understand that you're president of the college, you're going to have a college. Is it going to be any good? Cause I don't want to waste my time.' 'Well, yes,' he says, 'Of course it's going to be good . . .' They didn't know where it was going to be, and they didn't know what they were going to call it."

—IRV CROSS, member of the first class of Long Beach State students

"I went out to enroll, and there was a fruit stand that was not being used to sell fruit. That was the information desk. It was at the corner of Anaheim and Pacific Coast Highway. The big classes were in the living room, and the middle size classes were in the dining room—in the bedrooms, and then the dining rooms . . . quite small. And the smallest classes were in the kitchens. And you would see people going through classrooms to get to the bathroom. And also the workmen were always coming through your classes. People ask me today, 'How come they call them the 49ers?' And I said, 'Because the school started in 1949. What better?' And then you ask about the colors. The gold is for the 49ers—the 'gold seekers.' And the brown is for the earth . . . And then we named the paper *Forty-Niner*. And we named the first yearbook *The Prospector*."

—FROM A 1987 INTERVIEW WITH ISABEL PATTERSON, one of the first students. (The school colors would later be changed to black and gold.) She would become a philanthropist whose donation made the Isabel Patterson Child Development Center possible.

- ELECTION CANDIDATES LINED UP -

THE 49er

VOL. 2—NO. 2 Long Beach State College, Long Beach, California FRIDAY, OCTOBER 6, 1950

COUNCIL CALLS OPEN MEETING TO DECIDE COLLEGE TEAM NAME

ASSEMBLY CLIMAXES CONTEST

Climaxing the October 13 election race campus politicos will take the stand Monday at 10:50 a.m. in front of the library to make their final bids for the 21 vacancies in high student places. Sharing the spotlight will be the proposed amendment to the student body constitution as speakers present their arguments for and against the measure.

(Continued to page 3)

FIELD HOOP TEAM THIS SEASON

WE COME TO a tense moment in the mock heroic epic put on by the WSOS last Friday for "Hello Day" entertainment. Mona Jean Ripley, Villain, (right) is shown menacing the poor old plumber father, Beverly Harrold. This skit started off "Hello Day" festivities with the proper degree of hilarity. —(49er Photo by Polly Seely)

OPINIONS ASKED ON COLORS, ANNUAL NAME

One of the most important decisions in the history of the college will be made when interested students and faculty members gather in the student lounge Tuesday at 3 p.m. to discuss suggestions for school colors, team names, yearbook title, and mascot.

Stressing the importance of the impending decisions, Dean David L. Bryant stated, "The college will be known in the future by the names and symbols chosen at this meeting."

(Continued to Page 3)

Announce Health Service Available To Students

Fireside Chat

SOOY URGES ONE SEMESTER TERMS FOR A S OFFICERS

Student President Kirk Sooy advocates strongly the adoption of the proposed constitutional amendment providing for semester terms, for student officers, in his first "fireside chat," which he presents to the students of Long Beach college via the columns of the 49er.

Tom Hamilton Gets $150 PTA Scholarship

Two Students Give Pros and Cons of Semester Term Amendment

CAMPUS CALENDAR OF EVENTS

(Opposite page, top) Developer Lloyd Whaley, who provided the campus with its temporary location in 1949, presents President P. Victor Peterson with a $1,000 stone marker for the college entrance in 1958.

(Opposite page, bottom.) Two of the first students, Roger Bryson and Joanne St. Louis stroll out of apartment classrooms in fall 1949. Bryson was the first student body president.

LONG BEACH
STATE COLLEGE

STATE COLLEGE
5401 EAST ANAHEIM STREET

1950s

THE MAKESHIFT APARTMENTS WERE GETTING CRAMPED by the early fifties, the classes running till ten every night, including Saturday. After getting the voters' blessing for a new campus, construction started on barracks-like structures that would be the college's new temporary quarters so facilities could be constructed on the new Long Beach State campus. Even with chaos, and classes in temporary structures, students tried to construct college life of a sort. They created a yearbook in 1950, started student activities like the annual 49er Days event as well as an "Evenings on Campus" series to inject a little culture into the new college experience.

Groundbreaking for the permanent buildings begins in 1953. P. Victor Peterson is fourth from left. Florence Bixby, the wife of landowner Fred Bixby, is in the center.

They may call it by a variety of uninviting names; but the food served up in the Forty-Niner canteen fills the need, judging from the waiting lines between classes and the healthy look of the students. Coffee, tea, Forty-Niner punch, sandwiches, shakes, cookies and coke. You name it; and if they haven't got it they'll sell you something else. But whatever it is, it will be served with a smile.

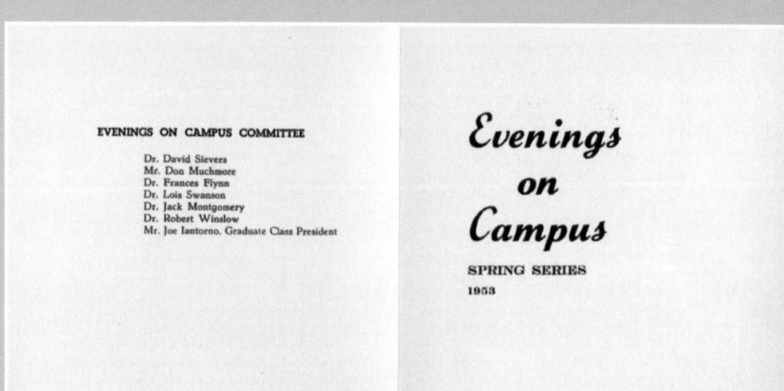

EVENINGS ON CAMPUS COMMITTEE

Dr. David Sievers
Mr. Don Muchmore
Dr. Frances Flynn
Dr. Lois Swanson
Dr. Jack Montgomery
Dr. Robert Winslow
Mr. Joe Iantorno, Graduate Class President

Please place me on your mailing list for future events at Long Beach State College.

Name ______________________

Address ______________________

City ______________ State ________

Evenings on Campus

SPRING SERIES
1953

STATE COLLEGE
LONG BEACH
'49er PLAYHOUSE

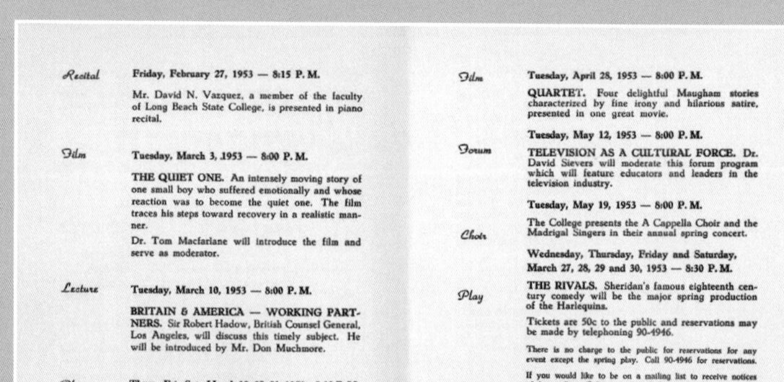

Recital — **Friday, February 27, 1953 — 8:15 P. M.**

Mr. David N. Vazquez, a member of the faculty of Long Beach State College, is presented in piano recital.

Film — **Tuesday, March 3, 1953 — 8:00 P. M.**

THE QUIET ONE. An intensely moving story of one small boy who suffered emotionally and whose reaction was to become the quiet one. The film traces his steps toward recovery in a realistic manner.

Dr. Tom Macfarlane will introduce the film and serve as moderator.

Lecture — **Tuesday, March 10, 1953 — 8:00 P. M.**

BRITAIN & AMERICA — WORKING PARTNERS. Sir Robert Hadow, British Counsel General, Los Angeles, will discuss this timely subject. He will be introduced by Mr. Don Muchmore.

Plays — **Thurs., Fri., Sat., March 19, 20, 21, 1953—8:30 P. M.**

Three One Acts

FRESH VARIABLE WINDS by Nora Stirling. This play, written for the National Committee for Mental Hygiene, is being presented for the California Congress of Parents and Teachers Convention.

THE RISING OF THE MOON by Lady Gregory.

THE FARCE OF MASTER PIERRE PATELIN. A medieval farce.

Chamber Music — **Tuesday, April 21, 1953 — 8:15 P. M.**

A program of chamber music featuring original compositions by Dr. Richard Hervig and Dr. Bertram McGarrity.

Film — **Tuesday, April 28, 1953 — 8:00 P. M.**

QUARTET. Four delightful Maugham stories characterized by fine irony and hilarious satire, presented in one great movie.

Forum — **Tuesday, May 12, 1953 — 8:00 P. M.**

TELEVISION AS A CULTURAL FORCE. Dr. David Sievers will moderate this forum program which will feature educators and leaders in the television industry.

Choir — **Tuesday, May 19, 1953 — 8:00 P. M.**

The College presents the A Cappella Choir and the Madrigal Singers in their annual spring concert.

Play — **Wednesday, Thursday, Friday and Saturday, March 27, 28, 29 and 30, 1953 — 8:30 P. M.**

THE RIVALS. Sheridan's famous eighteenth century comedy will be the major spring production of the Harlequins.

Tickets are 50c to the public and reservations may be made by telephoning 90-4946.

There is no charge to the public for reservations for any event except the spring play. Call 90-4946 for reservations.

If you would like to be on a mailing list to receive notices of future State College events which are open to the public, please tear off coupon below and mail to:

ACTIVITIES OFFICE
LONG BEACH STATE COLLEGE
6201 East Anaheim Road
Long Beach 15, California

Student life revolves about the "quad".

P. VICTOR PETERSON—NAMESAKE OF PROSPECTOR PETE

P. Victor Peterson was a large, imposing man who favored double-breasted suits and was rarely seen in shirtsleeves. The Iowa native did not seem like a man to lead the messy launch of Los Angeles-Orange County State College.

But he did. Peterson took the college from apartment houses to the temporary structures on lower campus to the earliest permanent buildings on a barren 322-acre expanse.

He was the namesake of the former mascot, Prospector Pete, and he saw the first science buildings named after him. Years after he retired, Peterson could be seen strolling through 49er Days, the Old West college social event, with a cowboy hat and plastic holster and guns.

"He didn't have the kind of outgoing, charming personality associated with university presidents," said Lee Brown, who graduated with a journalism degree in 1960. "But he was a builder."

As president, Peterson scoured the country looking for faculty for the new college. He said in an oral history recorded in 1971 that he interviewed faculty to get "their philosophy of life. I tried to figure out, near as I could . . . if they were a decent sort and whether they could fit into this kind of an institution."

Born in 1892 in Hampton, Iowa, Peterson served in the United States Army Medical Corps in World War I. He taught chemistry and agriculture before moving to San Jose State College. He taught chemistry there as well and became a dean of the college.

P. Victor Peterson, (on ladder) poses with faculty and local officials when Long Beach State College becomes official in June 1950.

He also chaired the San Jose City planning commission from 1939 to 1947. His daughter, Ellie Johnson, said her father favored hilltop locales, which factored into the selection of the Long Beach college site—which was set on a hill on what was then the outskirts of town.

Peterson's planning commission experience drew the attention of state officials, who convinced Peterson to serve as interim president of Los Angeles State College in 1947, and help establish Los Angeles-Orange County State College two years later. Indeed, at Long Beach, Peterson ruled with an iron fist. He personally recruited and hired faculty, and all decisions went through his office.

Peterson felt professors should focus their time on the classroom and students. Francis "Frenchy" Flynn, a longtime dean at the college in the fifties and sixties, said later that Peterson and most administrators at the time believed the state colleges should be "basically geared to the vocational and the occupational," and that research and advanced degrees should be left to the University of California schools.

Shared governance that put faculty in the mix of decision-making was not happening, certainly not at Long Beach State in the 1950s.

As the decade rolled on, faculty were growing increasingly restive. They wanted a voice in decision-making, and many sought to pursue a more ambitious curriculum beyond broad survey courses and teacher training. The administrators, who were under pressure to grow a college quickly, were butting heads with young faculty members who had enough chutzpah to move across the country to a Southern California college no one had heard of.

Eventually, things got difficult.

By 1959, almost 60 percent of the faculty he had hired wanted Peterson to resign. Peterson, a staunch Republican, alleged that a "left-wing

An early 1950s plans for the temporary facilities on lower campus. The barracks-like buildings would be used for decades while permanent buildings gradually took shape on upper campus. President P. Victor Peterson spent much of his time overseeing unending campus construction projects.

Students pose by the temporary buildings on lower campus in the early 1950s.

element" had infiltrated, while faculty said people were being dismissed on trumped-up charges for challenging the administration. Bill O'Neill, a student in the college's first class who returned to teach in the late fifties, later described an atmosphere of professors "locked in offices, drinking coffee, and smoking and plotting against the administration."

The fight was by then drawing notice in the media. "LBSC Prexy Under Fire, Won't Quit," read one *Los Angeles Times* headline. More importantly, the campus brouhaha was getting attention from Sacramento as professors traveled north to complain.

Peterson retired June 30, 1959, at age 67.

Flynn, the former dean, said later that while he supported Peterson's decisions, he had to admit that administrators at the college in the fifties "were probably not bringing faculty into the decision-making as well as we should have, I'm sure of that."

Richard Wilde, one of the professors most staunchly opposed to Peterson's policies, wrote, years later, that he gave Peterson credit for using his knowledge of the complex state system to "build a California state college out of nothing. He was definitely right in insisting that faculty give first priority to teaching, though wrong in denigrating scholarship and research." Wilde said that Peterson "rightly aimed to avoid an undergraduate education evident at major universities where faculty, focused on research, had little direct contact with undergraduates."

For the next twenty years, Peterson was active in college and city affairs, including 49er Days. He died in 1979. College president Stephen Horn said then that Peterson "had the dedication and energy to begin . . . a great university and to live to see it well underway in meeting the great needs of a diverse regional, national, and international population."

Students gather in Los Cerritos in 1961. Then a women's dorm, the hall had strict curfews—no men after 10 p. m.

LONG BEACH
STATE COLLEGE
49-ERS

President P. Victor Peterson (seated in the center) poses with college deans, architects, and local politicians to mark the start of fresh construction on the new campus in the early 1950s.

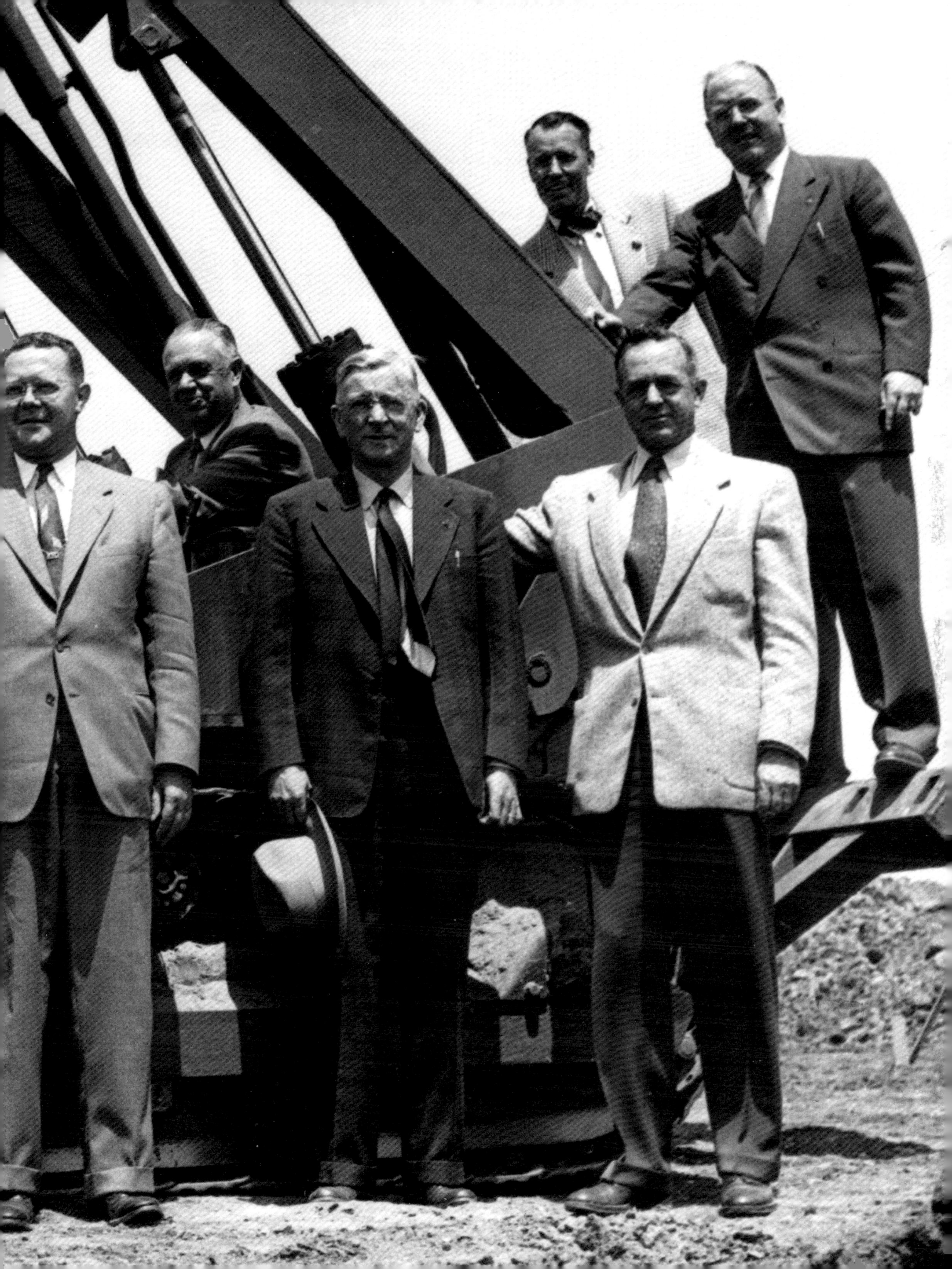

BEVERLY (LEWIS) O'NEILL

"WE WERE IN THE BEGINNING OF SOMETHING THAT WAS GOING TO GROW"

Beverly Lewis, who would go on to be a popular three-term mayor of Long Beach, went to Long Beach State in the early 1950s because she had no other choice.

" . . . Long Beach State was an answer I had at the time—and the only one—because there just wasn't funding to go someplace where it was going to be costly," she said years later.

USC and UCLA were out of the question. Her father told her to take up typing.

The future mayor was one of the first students at the new college. She met her husband, Bill O'Neill, there, and when they got married, several professors came to the wedding.

She remembers stepping over mud between classes in the temporary buildings and running out of class once or twice to rescue her car, when it slid in the mud in the campus parking lot on a rainy day. Despite the challenges, O'Neill loved going to school in those early days.

"I felt like we were building something," she said. "It was exciting; we were in the beginning of something that was going to grow."

College librarian, Charles Boorkman, inspects the construction site for the new library annex, as a pile driver sinks supports into the ground.

Library increases services, facilities

A place to listen to a favorite symphony, to study for finals, to type a term paper, or to provide shelter from the rain – the library is many things to many people.

The library employs more than 100 full-time staff members and 230 student assistants to make its many services available. Among these services are filmstrips, records, tapes, pamphlets, magazines, newspapers, and all kinds of microtexts; also curriculum guides, teaching aids (from scientific scale models to band instruments for elementary teaching), and, of course, books.

Aside from valuable service to research, the Library provides other tools of the educational process, such as copy machines, typewriters, conference rooms, listening rooms, and taped programs during certain hours.

Last summer, construction began on a six-story library annex which should be completed by the fall of 1970. New features of the annex will include a multi-media unit, which will house two elevated viewing lecture halls. These will feature television, motion pictures, and slide viewing.

Other innovations will be a facility to record lectures and a computer testing device for the classroom. The annex will more than double present library seating capacity and floor space.

Finding a solitary corner in the stacks, coed settles down for study.

CHARLES BOORKMAN

"BEAUTIFULLY EXPLOSIVE" LIBRARIAN

Librarian Charles Boorkman, the third person to be hired by the college, was a "beautifully explosive person who was always going in the right direction," noted Floyd Erickson in a testimonial to Boorkman, with whom he worked. Boorkman would rail at the chancellor's office for not being attentive enough to the library's needs. He could also be moved literally to tears by a sad story.

When classes at the new college started in 1949, there wasn't a single book. When funds were acquired to purchase the first book, which arrived on December 15, 1949, it was "a red-letter day for the library," Boorkman noted in a campus history. He oversaw the construction of the first library building—essentially a large wooden shack—by the campus apartments. In 1951, the building was moved, shelves and all, so crammed with recently acquired volumes that nothing budged as they rumbled up the hill to the new campus. He oversaw the building of the first small library among the temporary buildings and then, much later, the five-story library at its present location.

Hamstrung by a lack of money in the early days, Boorkman acted quickly when money started flowing in the early sixties. Boorkman and his staff would eventually acquire more than one million volumes, including rare finds by D. H. Lawrence and Robinson Jeffers and the MGM Library of Music. He obtained Dorothy Healey's collection of radical literature, brushing aside intense criticism. He outmaneuvered other buyers to obtain the famous Phil Bekeart collection of Californiana.

"He built that library up from nothing," said former library dean Roman Kochan, who was hired by Boorkman in the sixties. Kochan remembers Boorkman in his office, working under clouds of cigarette smoke, and a gruff exterior that masked a big heart.

He could also be stubborn, where his books were concerned.

"He defied opposition by purchasing controversial material and making it freely available," Jacob Zeitlin said at Boorkman's 1976 retirement. Zeitlin, an LA-based rare bookseller and appraiser, recalled that when someone complained about the *Dictionary of Modern Slang*, Boorkman answered, "Yes, it's on an open shelf, and there it will stay and it's none of anybody's damn business!"

He also went beyond books and was one the first college librarians to buy audiovisual equipment and materials.

Boorkman played the violin and had deep interests in numerous subjects, including Egyptian archaeology. He was also a gourmet cook who had an "addiction" to reading, friends say. He was in the midst of *Manchester's Last Lion* when he died in 1983.

"There are treasures in there that people don't even know about, and it's all thanks to Charlie," said Kochan, who used to accompany Boorkman on his trips to rare-book dealers in Los Angeles.

Students spend a profitable hour in the reserve reading room.

Charles Boorkman (second from right) poses with other administrators in the modest temporary library in the early 1950s.

JOHN MCCONNELL

"I'D HAVE ANSWERED YES TO ANYTHING!"

John McConnell was thirty when President P. Victor Peterson interviewed him about a job teaching PE and coaching the new college's first baseball team. McConnell was thrilled at the chance to leave Iowa and move to the Golden State.

"Peterson was conducting a series of interviews, and I was one of the ones in the late afternoon. I remember one of the questions—'Do you think you could give leadership to the baseball program?' I'd have answered yes to anything! Nuclear physics if he asked."

The interview was brief, and Peterson kept looking at his watch. He found out later the president was trying to catch the last train out of Iowa City.

In fall 1953, after driving west with his wife and young sons, McConnell would learn just how new this California college was.

"It was such a shock," McConnell said. "Nobody told us it [the program] was only a few years old . . . There were only two buildings going up. One was the first segment of the PE facility." Sheep grazed on the new field on the barren, overgrown lower campus, and the new coach realized all the team's games would be away games.

Decades before the team would become known as the Dirtbags and players would become locally famous—and frequently drafted into the majors—McConnell's team experienced a rocky first season.

"I thought we started a year too soon. I had fourteen players," McConnell said. "[Coaches today] have a roster of about thirty. Several of the kids on the roster . . . I was afraid to play a couple of 'em. They weren't very good, and really I was afraid they would get hurt. I brought a kid in to pinch-run just to get him in the game. A ground ball was hit, and he had to go from first to second, and you always slide into second. Well, he went in standing up, and the

The baseball team started play in 1954 under John McConnell.

throw just hit him in the head. The ball went up in the air and took a while to come down."

McConnell coached through 1959 before going on to become PE director and administrator. His first-year salary was $4,740. In six years, he compiled an 86-65 record, but his first team won just three of sixteen games.

"We had nothing to offer in terms of recruitment. Some of the guys would get on-campus jobs, but that was it. Our field was set up so there were weeds in foul territory. After practice, we'd form a skirmish line and look for lost baseballs in the weeds," he said, laughing. "It was pretty primitive."

ROBERT E. VIVIAN

Robert E. Vivian helped grow the USC engineering program during World War II. After, while he was checking out the newish College of Engineering at Los Angeles State College and considering a job there, he got a call from Long Beach State. The 11-year-old Long Beach college had no engineering program and wanted to start one—with Vivian's help.

Vivian toured the campus, including the temporary, barracks-like buildings still in use while new structures were going up on the upper campus. He saw some potential, and he felt simpatico with Dean Robert Rhodes and President P. Victor Peterson.

"I was pleased with what I saw and the general atmosphere of the educational program there and with the interviews I had with Dean Rhodes and President P. Victor Peterson," he wrote later, for an early history of the engineering department. "Both of these men were scientists by education as well as administrators and experienced teachers, so I felt at home with them, and we understood each other . . ."

He signed on at Long Beach State, with the promise to offer senior classes by September 1959 and the first degrees by June 1960. The development of the program would signal a departure from the "teacher training" ethos that had guided the college since its founding. He used his connections to hire faculty and helped grow the program to 653 students by 1961. A new, three-story building went up in the spot once covered by barracks scrub. Then Douglas Aircraft asked the college to provide an MS program for employees.

Vivian, who went on to help other California college engineering programs, retired from LBSU in 1964, and the next year was honored with the statue of The Bent of Tau Beta Pi and later the Vivian Engineering Center.

(Opposite page) Retired Dean Robert E. Vivian (left) at dedication of the "Bent," National Engineering Honor Society, in 1966.

THE BENT OF TAU BETA PI
National Engineering Honor Society
Dedicated in Honor of
ROBERT E. VIVIAN
Dean Emeritus of Engineering
California State College
at Long Beach
CALIFORNIA THETA CHAPTER
Established 30 January 1965

Looking northwest from Hardfact Hill in 1957, now the site of the Hall of Science.

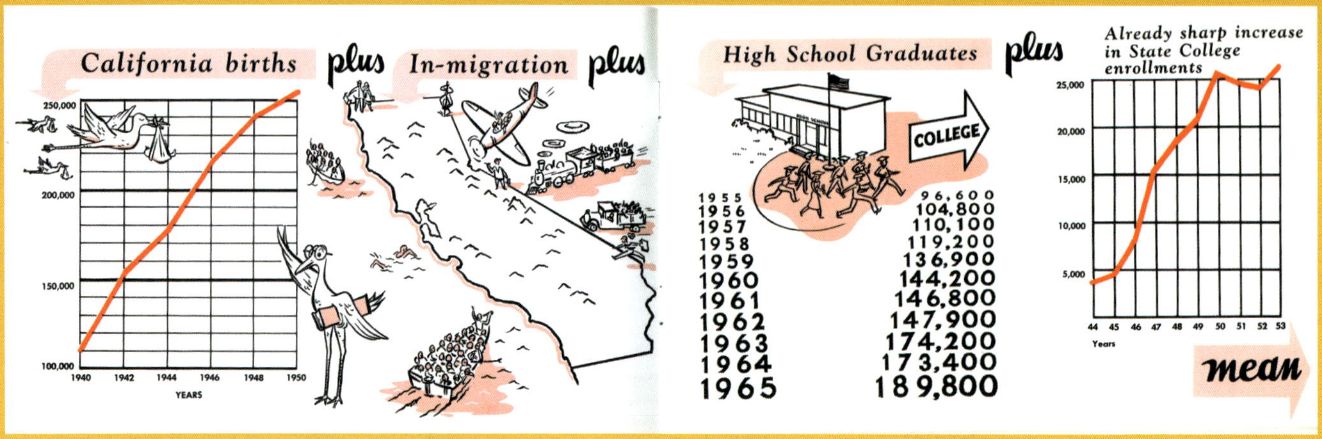

CALIFORNIA MUST ACT NOW!
THE JOB CANNOT BE DONE IN ONE YEAR.

To provide the necessary facilities for the state colleges . . .

$24,000,000 IS REQUIRED IN 1954 and
$24,000,000 EVERY YEAR THEREAFTER

The longer we wait the greater our backlog of need – and the harder the problem!

Will California measure up to this great need?

Support your legislator as he constructively meets this grave and vital problem.

Don't deny your child the opportunity for a college education!

In the 1950s, Long Beach State, like a lot of California schools, was scrambling to accommodate the deluge of students and the looming baby boomer "burst rate." This eventually led to the creation of the 1960 Master Plan for Higher Education, which mapped out the University of California, Cal State, and community college systems with the idea that education should be for all. The plan led to a boost in development for higher education statewide, including at Long Beach State. Tuition was free for many years, but that would not last.

WITH THESE FACILITIES NOW

827 CLASSROOMS

We must have this addition by 1958

541 + 827 CLASSROOMS

These will barely serve the students by 1962

538 + 541 + 827 CLASSROOMS

1965 calls for . . .

502 + 538 + 541 + 827 CLASSROOMS

It takes time to build . . .

Funds appropriated	Plans approved	Construction begins	Building completed
Say: June 1, 1954	Oct. 20, 1955	Feb. 1, 1956	Sept. 1, 1957

TOTAL TIME ELAPSED . . . . 3 YEARS, 2 MONTHS (often longer)

therefore:

Funds provided by Legislature in . . .

Will provide classrooms not earlier than . . .

SPRING	SEPT.
1954	1957
1955	1958
1956	1959
1957	1960
1958	1961
1959	1962
1960	1963
1961	1964
1962	1965

After 1958 THE PRESSURE *gets worse!*

FOR EVERY STUDENT IN STATE COLLEGES TODAY (1954) THERE WILL BE . . . .

1.5	STUDENTS IN		1958
1.6	"	"	1959
1.8	"	"	1960
1.9	"	"	1961
2.0	"	"	1962
2.2	"	"	1963
2.3	"	"	1964
2.4	"	"	1965

1954

1965

California's young people want and deserve a college education.

Their parents demand it for them because they know that college education means progress and leadership.

Public schools need thousands of teachers and the State Colleges are a principal source of supply.

Trained men and women are needed for: BUSINESS, INDUSTRY, and PUBLIC SERVICE.

DEMOCRACY IS BASED UPON AN EDUCATED CITIZENRY!

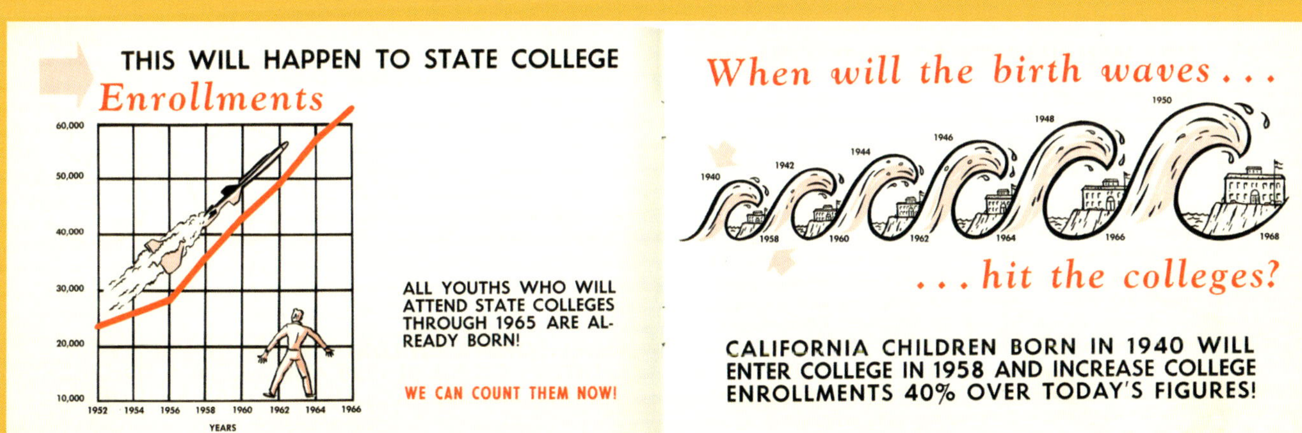

THIS WILL HAPPEN TO STATE COLLEGE *Enrollments*

ALL YOUTHS WHO WILL ATTEND STATE COLLEGES THROUGH 1965 ARE ALREADY BORN!

WE CAN COUNT THEM NOW!

When will the birth waves . . .

. . . hit the colleges?

CALIFORNIA CHILDREN BORN IN 1940 WILL ENTER COLLEGE IN 1958 AND INCREASE COLLEGE ENROLLMENTS 40% OVER TODAY'S FIGURES!

LEE BROWN

Lee Brown was working at Douglas Aircraft and living in a trailer on his parents' Lakewood Village property in the early 1950s when a chance encounter led him first to the United States Air Force, then free college on the G.I. Bill at Long Beach State, and later, grad school. He would work for the university PR department after his 1960 graduation before joining the *Long Beach Press-Telegram*. Brown returned as a journalism professor in the 1990s. A chance encounter decided his military service and, in a sense, his own path.

He was taking trash out to the alley when he saw a guy about his age across the way taking out his own trash. Brown went over to shake hands to introduce himself and realized the neighbor didn't have any. "What he had were these hooks," Brown recalled. "He had been in Korea and had both hands shot off. His detachment left him there in the snow and the Marines got him out . . . I knew right then I did not want to go to Korea."

Brown signed up for the Air Force instead and was sent to Texas, and when he was discharged, he was eager to use his G.I. Bill money to take journalism classes. He remembered a small Long Beach campus with parking problems and a very active Greek life—dances and sock hops and a Spring Sing.

Brown wasn't interested in that; he wanted to become a journalist and became editor of the *Forty-Niner*. In a sense he saw the coming of age of Long Beach State.

"The dorms were built under President Peterson. He was a builder. Building, building, building. I mean, we're just growing by leaps and bounds," Brown said. "One time, a year or two after I graduated, registration was in person. And you met somebody, and you signed up for your class. It lasted till almost midnight. And President [Carl] McIntosh, the second president, almost went nuts when that happened because he thought that was god-awful. And it was."

(Opposite page, bottom) The campus from above in the mid 1950s.

NO END IN SIGHT—Long, and getting longer, is class card line stretching across campus.

February rains force College Union groundbreaking into the Cafeteria for a symbolic turning of dirt. Taking part are Lyal Leibrock, Marvin Haney, Edward Killingsworth, architect; Rex Gay, A.S. president; Colleen Bentley, and Howard Adler, former A.S. president. Nap Harris (right) looks on approvingly.

Two workmen inspect the skeletal forms an reinforcements of the Library annex.

After years of planning, the real ground breaking for the College Union begins amid smoke of red flares and heavy rains late in February, 1969.

1960s

THE CAMPUS GREW IN EVERY POSSIBLE WAY IN THE SIXTIES: new buildings—including a University Student Union—new trees, music, and increasing activism for growing numbers of Black, Chicano, and Asian students. There were new fees, too, to build the University Student Union that would eventually help unify the campus.

GARY LITTLE

Gary Little arrived in 1962 and was student government president and sports editor of the *Forty-Niner* before going on to serve as an administrator, including as director of student housing. But first he was a big man on campus at the young Long Beach State. Some of his favorite memories involve watching basketball at the old Gold Mine Gym.

"When [Jerry] Tarkanian coached, it was exciting," Little recalled." It was probably a liability, but when you walked in, they handed you wooden blocks. And you'd bang them together. It was fun."

Little remembers a barren, but friendly, campus when he arrived. He carpooled to school with the football players, and he himself ran cross-country despite being told he couldn't because he'd had rheumatic fever and a heart murmur.

"I went up to Jack Rose [the namesake of the Jack Rose Track]. and he had a lot of positive energy. I met one of the track guys, Bill Tillney, who was the AS president. I was the parliamentarian of the student senate. We had all kinds of combinations of students. Some transferred. Some came because it was local and affordable."

Football games, 49er Days, homecoming parades through Belmont Shore, and the Spring Sing were all a big deal on campus and Little went to everything.

GARRY LITTLE and Dean Lois Swanson meet on campus on the way to a conference about the agenda for the coming meeting of the President's Council.

FORMING A BLOCK LBS, the band salutes the rooting section during its halftime show at the Fresno football game.

Spirited Marching Band Adds Pep to LBSC

The first football team suited up in 1955 under coach Mike DeLotto.

"We had a really excellent marching band in those days. We were playing Cal Poly—they were highly ranked and we upset them. A group of us marched downtown to the *Press-Telegram* to see sportswriter Hank Hollingsworth; he was always really hard on Long Beach State. We had a spontaneous demonstration at the PT calling for Hollingsworth. There were hundreds of us. But he wasn't there. We had the whole intersection blocked off on Pine Avenue."

JON REGNIER

"IT WAS A FUN TIME."

In April 1966, 28-year-old Jon Regnier had a new baby at home, and his shop teacher job would no longer cover the bills. With a background in architecture, he managed to get hired as a building coordinator at Long Beach State, the school where he earned his teaching credentials. Back then, the 15-year-old Long Beach State campus was stark, nearly treeless, and desperately in need of a building boom to accommodate the baby boomers who were streaming in.

His first challenge: the state's top-down approval system for building anything for the cost-conscious Cal State system. That's how concrete facades came to be at Sacramento State, Northridge, and even Long Beach. The legislative analyst in Sacramento once told him, "Jon, you gotta understand, it's not how much they cost; they gotta look cheap!" Taxpayers might complain to the legislature if they saw anything but concrete at the state institutions, the thinking went.

Later on, Regnier would become something of a wheeler-dealer who helped get the growing college the infrastructure it desperately needed. When Regnier wanted fifteen-gallon Ficus trees—five over the limit allowed by the state—he traded equipment with Cal Trans to get the bigger trees they had. Regnier and his crew lobbied the city to install a traffic light on Seventh Street by the college entrance, to no avail. Then a Cal Trans engineer mentioned he had a nephew who wanted to get into Long Beach State. Calls were made to President Carl McIntosh and the college had its traffic light.

Isabel Patterson, the Realtor and alumna whose contribution made the Isabel Patterson Child Development Center (CDC) possible, turned the tables on Regnier, who by then was divorced and was dating center director Pamela Macdonald. Patterson was

Architect Kenny Wing Jr., state senator (later governor) George Deukmejian, director of physical planning and development Jon Regnier and President Steve Horn breaking ground on the addition to the health services building in 1975.

getting impatient with college officials, like Regnier, who she felt were dragging their feet on adding an infant and toddler center to the CDC. Patterson told Regnier, "Pamela won't marry you until you build that." They did wed in 1999, and the infant and toddler center was built in 1994.

Regnier would go on to work in campus development and eventually at the CSU chancellor's office. Regnier had a hand on most big projects on campus. These included the College of Business Administration, which came to be after he drew the plans on a napkin while dining with the building architect at Hofs Hut. He helped get Brotman Hall built in the 1970s, as well as the pedestrian bridge from Brotman to the art gallery. He gave a boost to funding for the Social Sciences Public Administration (SSPA) building on lower campus after Willie Brown, then chairman of the Legislature's Ways and Means Committee, transferred the funding line to Dominguez Hills in the seventies. Regnier also helped create the three-court design for the Walter Pyramid and the hydraulic lift seats that preserved the hardwood floors. Said Regnier: "It was a fun time."

ROSEMARY TAYLOR SCHMIDT

In the early 1960s, Rosemary Taylor Schmidt danced as a saloon girl during the annual 49er Days celebration. When she became campus activities director, she taught college women how to properly walk through a receiving line. As fifties values evolved into the counterculture revolution, she had a front seat to the action.

Taylor Schmidt, who graduated in 1964, remembers the 49er Days, which started in the 1950s, when students labored all night to create prefabricated saloons and other gold rush ephemera and dress up in costumes to reenact the frenetic and crude days of the 1849 event that inspired the 49er namesake.

After working all night, revelers gathered at noon the next day, when the honorary sheriff cut the ribbon and 49er Days was on. It was crazy fun, but at times played into racist stereotypes about Mexican and Chinese people and Native Americans. Taylor Schmidt looked back at those days feeling "stultifying stupid about the world . . . then, you didn't think about your place in the world. The '50s were like that." The annual event would fade out by the 1970s.

As the sixties marched on, she and her colleagues could feel a change coming. Taylor Schmidt started working for the popular Lois Swanson, the associate dean of student affairs, who helped establish the campus's Greek system, student government, and a host of activities. The Greek system would come under fire over its policies on admitting Black students and others. Campus protests were becoming more frequent, and students started demanding an education focus beyond the white European model that predominated.

Taylor Schmidt escorted an exhausted Angela Davis to a speaking event after convincing the activist to take a snooze on her office couch. She remembers watching Joan Baez and Jefferson Airplane perform on Hardfact Hill, by what is now the Hall of Science. And then, in 1968, the Spater guerrilla art exhibit and subsequent controversy made Taylor Schmidt's life even more interesting. (See pages 61–63.)

"It was a very conservative campus," she said later. "It wasn't a campus out of LA, like UCLA. But it did have its spunk."

THE ARRIVAL OF EOP

The Educational Opportunity Program (EOP) was started in 1967 by Long Beach State professor Joseph White to help promising minority and low income students on campus with admissions support and financial aid. He launched the outreach program and worked with legislators to win state funding. Long Beach State's EOP became a model for other CSUs.

ANNA NIETOGOMEZ

Anna NietoGomez, a Latina sociology major, came to campus in 1967 and immediately felt isolated. She said one professor ignored her questions, and another told her it was pointless to instruct her because she would likely drop out and have children. Her life changed when she spotted a picket sign on campus that said, *CHICANO*. She became one of the first Chicana activists on campus, founding the Chicana feminist newspaper *Hijas de Cuauhtémoc* as well as becoming a recruiter for the EOC program that was instrumental in bringing people of color to campus.

"So I go to the history of the *Forty-Niner* and look at '67 and then look at the fall of '68. Look at the difference. There's pictures of minorities, wherever you see it's a mix, you see white students, Black students, Brown students. I took a picture of it because I said what a change. Wherever we, wherever you went, you saw a diverse group of people of color. Just the semester before it was all white. That's how transformative it was.

You know, I go to Cal State Long Beach now and it's commonplace. That was within my time, I was on campus and that was not coming. I hungered to see people from my community because I came from a segregated town . . . Your communities, they will talk to you, but white people didn't necessarily talk to you. It really created isolation. So those white people who did talk to you, they're the ones who kept me going. I owe a lot to them. Because they helped me . . . And they knew that there might be consequences if they did.

So my mom, we came in and got an apartment there in Belmont Shore. We had no idea what kind of community that was. I just wanted to live by the ocean. And we got an apartment. Then, I was supposed to come with a roommate from Stanford, . . . but she chickened out. But there was a girl there who took me to school. She worked at the drugstore and I bumped into her. She was a Chatty Cathy. She was very friendly. I was asking her about the bus lines. I learned she was going to Cal State Long Beach, too. And we found out that she lived around me and she had grown up there. And so she started giving me a ride to school. Bless her heart. She was a great, great, young woman. There were people who reached out to me and helped me and that's what helped me make it through 1967, so it was a world of contradiction. The aggressive hostilities were dominant . . . in the state of California.

ARMANDO VAZQUEZ-RAMOS

The 17-year-old did not know anyone going to college in 1967. Armando Vazquez-Ramos planned to go to LA Trade Tech and become an auto mechanic. He had a Jaguar he was working on, and he thought his future was set.

That's when he found out about Joseph White, who was recruiting Black and Chicano students for the Educational Opportunity Program at Long Beach State, including kids like him from Ramona Gardens in East LA. Then the LA walkouts happened, in 1968, as Chicano and Latino students protested being funneled into vocational programs and being reprimanded for speaking Spanish.

"It gave me . . . the first sense of purpose . . . a sense . . . I can make a difference," said Vazquez-Ramos. "And politics was never in my life. I was under a hood. And of course to me, it was essential." The walkouts, the "call for Chicano power and force," and demands to hire Mexican American teachers and counselors, coupled with the assassinations of the Rev. Martin Luther King Jr. and Sen. Robert Kennedy, galvanized Vazquez-Ramos.

He remembers marching in campus protests and dousing the Prospector Pete statue with brown paint more than once. "We were feeling our political oats . . . feeling that we could push to the limit wherever we could accomplish." By the time he graduated, in 1973, he was running the community-based organization El Centro de la Raza, otherwise known as the East Long Beach Neighborhood Center. He also cofounded the Chicano and Latino Studies Department at Long Beach State.

In the 2010s, Vazquez-Ramos led the fight to bring ethnic studies to California high schools. He also continues to lead a program to bring young California residents living there under the DACA

"Dreamer" Act to study abroad in Mexico and then bring them back to the US. By the time he started easing into retirement, Long Beach State was becoming a majority Latino campus.

Armando Vazquez-Ramos's 1973 wedding was held on the Long Beach State campus.

"Now you ask me, did I envision that? Hell no!" He's also not shy about criticizing the university for not hiring more Latino administrators in the upper echelons of the campus, and students for not raising more hell like he did in the sixties. "Why aren't they stopping the world, sitting in, fasting? They are sitting in the fold of the Democratic Party, and they've done nothing for us."

John McEuen's Willmore City Moonshiners didn't have much experience, but they were still regulars at The Golden Bear in Huntington Beach in the mid 1960s.

JOHN MCEUEN

It was at Long Beach State that future Grammy winner John McEuen learned math was not for him. The founding member of the Nitty Gritty Dirt Band came to campus with his high school pal Steve Martin, who, before he became a comedian and actor, was a philosophy major.

"I did ok in analytical trig . . . I was used to getting As and Bs . . . you actually had to study this stuff. The teacher said, 'Just remember it's only useful in the class; it has no usefulness in the outside world.' So why am I taking this class?"

McEuen stayed at the college from 1963–64. He'd take classes throughout the day and retreat to his car to nap and play his banjo, the instrument that would bring him renown and platinum records as a folk musician. McEuen would also hang out in the old McCabe's music store on Anaheim Street, sitting around the coffee table with other fellow musicians who would become the Nitty Gritty Dirt Band.

John McEuen, far right, with his first band, the Willmore City Moonshiners in Long Beach in 1964. The Garden Grove resident studied math at Long Beach State in the mid-1960s.

"I'd go there and practice and try to figure out what life was about . . . I'd drive down Highway 22, which was just done. My first guitar student was in Seal Beach. I had a dream life. I was going to college; I had a good school to go to. I'd do some of the assignments in the cafeteria with all the noise around me."

Martin, McEuen's friend, would later go on to fame as a stand-up comedian, *Saturday Night Live* regular, and movie and TV actor. McEuen, who at one time gave banjo lessons to his friend, would go on to a career in music. Neither man graduated from Long Beach State, though Martin would come back for his honorary degree in 1989.

McEuen wrote a term paper on the popular folk tune "Cripple Creek." He eventually took classes at Santa Ana Junior College. "That's when I found out I wasn't a math major for sure. I was in the music room, practicing, playing, and a final was coming up and . . . you can't cram calculus. I squeaked by with a D. I realized math wasn't my future unless it was percentage of the gate or something."

1965 INTERNATIONAL SCULPTURE SYMPOSIUM

The 1965 California International Sculpture Symposium was an ambitious plan to bring giant metal, wood, and concrete sculptures to the still-stark Long Beach State campus. The idea came from sculpture professor Kenneth Glenn, with backing from President Carl McIntosh and local architect Ed Killingsworth. The symposium drew artists from around the world, including Claire Falkenstein, who replaced an Italian artist who was injured in a car wreck in Europe. Her *U as a Set* still occupies the fountain by the McIntosh building.

The *Now* sculpture, by Piotr Kowalski, on the stairs leading to upper campus, was created by underwater exploding dynamite charges attached to sheets of steel. Once the structures started going up, the community got involved. Workers at the Naval shipyard and workers on campus had to make some finishing touches, as well.

(Opposite page) The Now sculpture takes shape near the future University Student Union.

PW218

Claire Falkenstein with her *U as a Set* sculpture.

Homage to Simon Rodia (builder of the Watts Towers) by J. J. Beljon, is still a feature by the Seventh Street entrance to the campus.

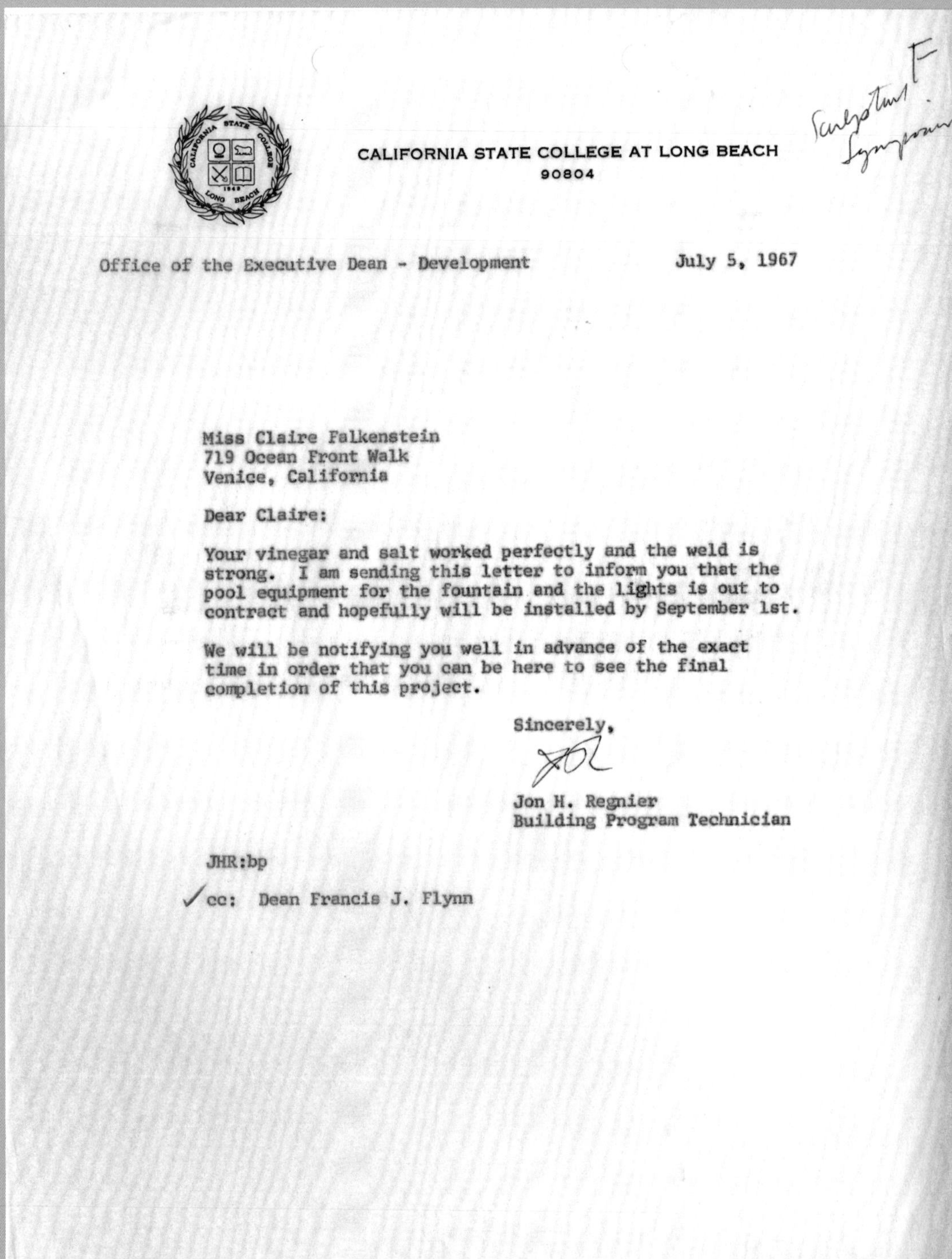

CALIFORNIA STATE COLLEGE AT LONG BEACH
90804

Office of the Executive Dean - Development July 5, 1967

Miss Claire Falkenstein
719 Ocean Front Walk
Venice, California

Dear Claire:

Your vinegar and salt worked perfectly and the weld is strong. I am sending this letter to inform you that the pool equipment for the fountain and the lights is out to contract and hopefully will be installed by September 1st.

We will be notifying you well in advance of the exact time in order that you can be here to see the final completion of this project.

Sincerely,

Jon H. Regnier
Building Program Technician

JHR:bp

cc: Dean Francis J. Flynn

THE SPATER EXHIBIT—CAMPUS OUTRAGE IN 1968

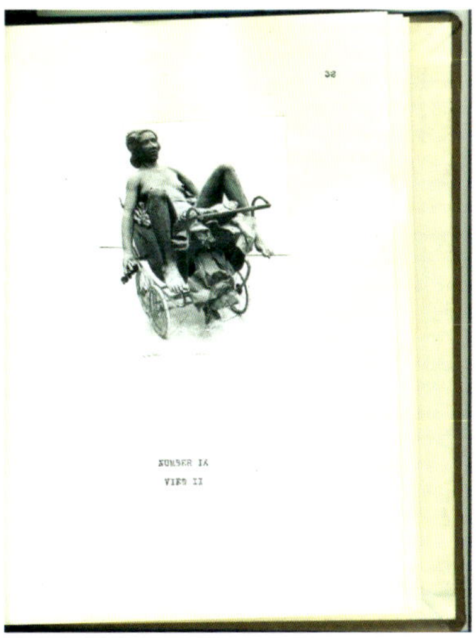

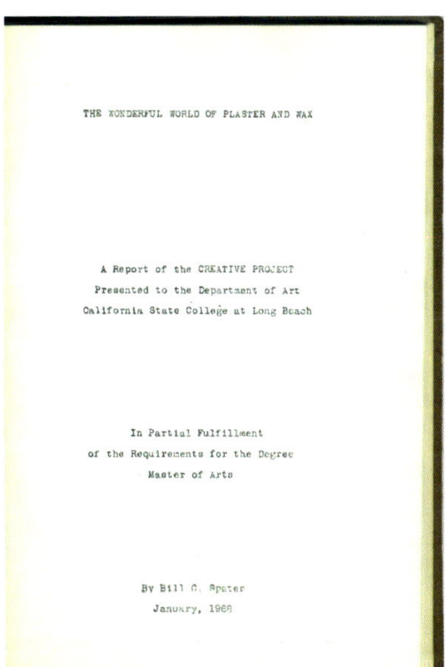

THE WONDERFUL WORLD OF PLASTER AND WAX

A Report of the CREATIVE PROJECT
Presented to the Department of Art
California State College at Long Beach

In Partial Fulfillment
of the Requirements for the Degree
Master of Arts

By Bill G. Spater
January, 1968

Graduate art student Bill Spater just wanted to get his graduate artwork displayed, as required for his thesis, which would be different from most of those filed at the university library. His ten larger-than-life statues depicted "the absurdity of our contemporary minds." He portrayed women straddling baby carriages and ironing boards and having intimate relations with television sets.

Campus officials dithered about giving him a chance to display before finally deciding not to. They awarded Spater his degree, but the work had not been shown, as was customary for master's students.

At 7 a.m. on April Fool's Day, 1968, Spater put his show on the upper campus lawn. Spater and his friends had dragged the statues out from the art room, roped them off, and stood guard. A bit later, activities director Rosemary Taylor Schmidt's phone rang.

"I scurried over to the grass out in front of the art department," she recalled later. "I walked up there and there was this life-size figure. There was a TV there and there was a guy's face inside the TV. There was a [statue of a] grown person standing outside the TV" with what might be called an essential body part inside. The statues were all over the lawn.

"It was very creative—kind of before its time."

A crowd of students formed, then a crowd of residents—about two thousand in all. Then the police came, and by midmorning, the show was over. The sculptures were removed from the lawn on orders from President Carl McIntosh.

Soon there were claims of artist censorship. Students posted photos of the statues on bulletin boards on campus. The police chief took them down. Professors posted photos of the statues in the same places. The police chief took them down. There were protests, demonstrations. A restricted, 18-and-over showing was scheduled for May.

But Cal State Chancellor Glenn Dumke canceled the exhibit, and then-Governor Ronald Reagan backed him, telling the *Forty-Niner* there was no need for "pornography" on campus. The move led to protests, a large police response, and forty-three arrests, one being a professor. The *Forty-Niner* claimed it was the first time that students were arrested for civil disobedience in the twenty-one-year history of the campus.

The actions led to lawsuits and more protests, but in the end, the guerrilla art show on the campus lawn was the only viewing Spater got for his work. The academic senate censured Dumke, and students contributed bail money for the jailed students. Summer break came, and students disappeared. Spater said he hadn't intended to create pornography for his graduate thesis, generating a free speech firestorm that swept the Long Beach State campus.

The Inglewood resident worked two-and-a-half years on his controversial sculptures. The work contained a touch of midcentury fantasy—a Venus rising from an ironing board, another woman with cowboy boots straddling an ironing board. He said later he wanted to be provocative. "I thought I was making something that would promote dialogue . . . something that was thought-provoking, not cheap or lurid. I was serious about it. As serious as a college student could be."

Spater was finishing his last piece, he said, when he believes someone noticed the exhibit in the sculpture lab and got it shut down. That's when he decided to haul the works onto the lawn. Fellow students came forward to help and tell the media about the free show.

Later, the chancellor quashed the compromise plan to exhibit the works. "That's when all hell broke loose," Spater recalled.

Bill Spater addresses students at a 1960s campus protest.

There were protests, arrests, and police in riot gear milling about the parking lot on Seventh Street south of campus. "I thought, this is getting too serious . . . way, way out of control. Considering the danger we presented as students it was an overreaction." He contends the whole thing would have blown over had the chancellor just allowed the exhibit to go on behind closed doors. Spater ended up suing, and the American Civil Liberties Union represented him. The long hours in court halls exposed him to new ideas and attorneys who became mentors. He later became an attorney with the California Appellate Project.

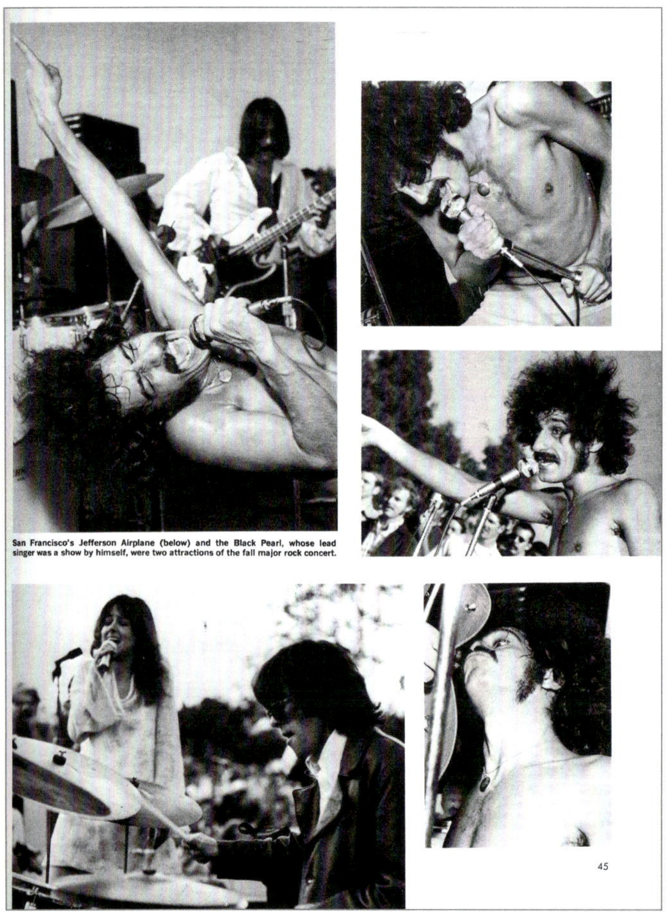
San Francisco's Jefferson Airplane (below) and the Black Pearl, whose lead singer was a show by himself, were two attractions of the fall major rock concert.

45

The "Spirit" beats drums.

Verbal and guitar sounds, electronically amplified, create a deafening rock at a weekly TGIF concert.

Campus is rocked by TGIF concerts

The whining of electrified sound pervaded the campus one Saturday early in November as the Jefferson Airplane, the San Francisco group famous for "Somebody to Love" and "White Rabbit," took off from the "Hardfact" sculpture area over the land of blues, folk, and rock, propelled by what they term "love rock."

The Airplane's departure from the campus green, accompanied by Spirit, Black Pearl, Chicago Transit Authority, and Collectors, was the first major Associated Students-sponsored rock concert at the college.

Throughout the year rock groups were audibly present at the "Now" sculpture almost every Friday noon. With names like Blues Image, General Store, Things to Come, and Cloud, they had come to celebrate TGIF (Thank God It's Friday).

Rock music can be an expression of both the performer and audience.

44

Grace Slick and Jefferson Airplane played on campus in the 1960s. So did The Doors. In 1989, Sublime was headlining at the Nugget Grill & Pub.

JEFFERSON AIRPLANE
CHICAGO TRANSIT AUTHORITY
THE COLLECTORS
AND OTHER HEAVY GROUPS
SPIRIT
9th of NOV.
NOON TILL MOON
TICKETS AVAILABLE AT
WALLACHS • USUAL GROOVY PLACES
TICKETS
AT THE GATE
How to Get there
Take the San Diego
Fwy to Bellflower
exit. Follow
Bellflower south
to Atherton st.
Turn left, special
signs will direct
you.
SATURDAY NOVEMBER 9th AT CAL. STATE LONG BEACH.

THE CARPENTERS

The legendary smooth-sound duo Richard and Karen Carpenter got their start at Long Beach State. Richard played piano and Karen loved playing drums and had to be coaxed to stand up on stage and sing. She did, with what *Rolling Stone* called a "chocolate and cream alto voice." The Carpenters gave budding comedian and fellow 49er Steve Martin his big break when they booked him as their opening act.

The Carpenters performed in the Long Beach State choir, led by director Frank Pooler, the turtleneck-sporting choral impresario who shaped the university choirs when he came to the college in the late 1950s.

Long Beach State choir director Frank Pooler.

Karen and Richard Carpenter with their mentor, Frank Pooler.

Pooler nurtured the Carpenters, encouraging them to try a blended sound, which they used to gold-record effect with "We've Only Just Begun" and "Superstar." He worked with Karen to extend her vocal range to make it even stronger for classical and pop songs. Pooler also cowrote "Merry Christmas, Darling" with Richard Carpenter.

The Carpenters performed in the Gold Mine gym as well as the Terrace Theater in Long Beach in 1978, which was Karen's final performance. Karen died in 1983. The Long Beach State choir sang at her funeral at a Downey church. Richard Carpenter donated funds to help create the Richard and Karen Carpenter Performing Arts Center on campus, which opened in 1994.

FRANK POOLER

"MORE MONEY FROM THIS SONG EVERY YEAR"

Frank Pooler taught music at CSULB from 1959 to 1988 and became perhaps best known as mentor to the Carpenters. "It's hard to find the words that say it strong enough," former student Frank DeWitt, a choral leader, told the *Long Beach Press-Telegram*, and that he was "the singular most significant person in our lives."

CSULB Choir Director Jonathan Talberg became friends with Pooler after Pooler retired and recalled his impact on the program many years later:

> He was an autodidact, a brilliant genius. Musician, artist, painter, collector of political memorabilia. A great storyteller jokester.
>
> . . . At a time when music was very regimented, and buttoned down, Frank was supportive of jazz, he had played jazz growing up. He was supportive of pop music, obviously, he had his relationship with the Carpenters. He was supportive of Richard finishing a degree at the same time as he was on the road.
>
> Choral music has always been tied to the church . . . Frank was not afraid to secularize choral music. He'd say "we're gonna still sing great music of the past but also, there's new interesting music that's non-sacred that's worth performing."
>
> He was a Pied Piper of people. People wanted to study with him. They wanted to be in his presence. He was fun. And he had a vision for touring.
>
> I was having lunch with Frank and it was the holidays. "Merry Christmas, Darling" came on the radio . . . And I asked about residuals for the song because I didn't know. He said, "Jon, I make more money on this song every year than I do on my retirement from Cal State Long Beach." And he retired as a full professor.

MWALIMU (DONNA) EVANS

When she was studying at Long Beach State in the 1960s, Donna (later Mwalimu) Evans said there were so few Black students on campus that "when we'd see each other, we'd run up to give each other a hug."

Evans graduated in 1968 after attending Compton College for two years and a trade school before coming to Long Beach State.

"I don't remember feeling I was unwelcome," said Evans, who was a recreation major. "I don't remember that anybody treated me badly."

She met up with Black students in a bungalow on upper campus and connected with members of the All-African People's Revolutionary Party.

Evans recalls speaking with Mexican American and Asian students as students of color fought to get recognition on what was then a largely white campus. "We knew it was important to fight, to push back.

"We'd go to student government meetings and protest. They saw our side of it, too. There were some *Forty-Niner* writers who saw our side of it." They organized, they went and made their voices heard at student government meetings. "We went to the student body meeting and one girl was putting on her makeup. We might have knocked stuff out of their hands, there's a picture of us standing behind white students. Our feeling was 'we're speaking, you're not going to do that.'"

After graduation she became a teacher. She taught in Long Beach and founded what became the Mandela Children's Learning Village in Compton. "It was a great time," at Long Beach State, she said. "I had fun and I had lots of friends."

Laura Terry—"This Is a New Time"

During her first semester, in 1966, Laura Terry (then Murphy) was approached by Professor Clyde Taylor about forming a Black student group they later named the Black Student Union. She graduated in 1971, later got her master's degree at Cal State LA, and taught in the Long Beach and Los Angeles districts.

"Dr. Taylor said we should conduct a student-wide election . . . we passed out flyers and met on upper campus in the administration building and proceeded to have an election of officers. A number of athletes joined the meeting—Clifton Marsh, Tony Wilkins, and others. Nominations were made and at the end Tony Wilkins was elected as the first BSU President. (Wilkins was shot and killed at the Hollywood Bowl in 1974 by a police officer working as a security guard.)

During the fall semester of 1966, I, along with a former schoolmate (Valerie Moreland a.k.a. Ayana) pledged Sigma Gamma Rho sorority, which was only a "colony" due to the college not giving it full campus charter status. Several other sororities left the campus in fear of Black girls pledging during Rush Week. They came back when they discovered we only wanted to join Sigma Gamma Rho, a national Black fraternal organization. Much later, the Omega and Kappa came on campus until finally all of the Divine Nine came on.

We were taking a class with Dr. Taylor. Dr. Joseph White (and first EOP director Ernie Clark) figured out a way to get Black kids on campus by using a technicality . . . that they used for athletes. He talked to the college president. He was instrumental in providing loans and grants. He was successful in getting sixty students and he was able to show they could survive on campus. They went out and started writing out a program, the Educational Opportunity Program. We used the program to get more students and got a grant.

President Carl McIntosh was really attuned to what we were doing; they wanted to hire more Black faculty and have more programs. We became volunteers to recruit new students.

We wanted our own department. We thought we were so big, bad, and bold. McIntosh wanted to meet with us, Donna and us two females. He talked to the men and the women were supposed to wait outside. Up until then we didn't notice all this chauvinistic stuff in the organization.

He [McIntosh] gave us everything we demanded—a work study position for the Black student office. It was an old faculty conference room with an old kitchenette. Some flower children painted in flowers and such and we had a fit. He told us all, you gotta take these new courses to the academic senate. We had to interview and hire . . . we said you gotta advertise in the right place, Black radio stations.

(Terry said her mother sometimes complained to her about her activism.)

She thought the radicals had got me. I'd tell her, "Mom this is the sixties and these are different kids . . . This is a new time. We are trying to get equal rights for Blacks."

“

I probably would have focused more on girls and women instead of politics my first year. I missed out on a lot of great socializing by being so politically active. By senior year I did have a couple fine girlfriends I liked a lot. I would have spent more time at Hussongs in Mexico rather than Prague and Vietnam. I was out trying to save the world. I should have been involved with socializing and revelry.

—Dana Rohrabacher, former US Representative and 1969 graduate

Growth, and the parking problems, continued unabated through the 1960s. Long Beach State College became California State College at Long Beach in 1964 before changing its name (slightly) in 1968 and again in 1972 to California State University, Long Beach.

A worker changes the sign on the Bellflower entrance in 1964.

Committee for Flowering Trees

At

California State College at Long Beach

726 EDISON BUILDING

100 LONG BEACH BLVD. • LONG BEACH, CALIFORNIA 90802

HEMLOCK 6-4456

LLEWELLYN BIXBY, JR.
Chairman

ROBERT L. IRVIN
Vice Chairman

WILLIAM CRAWFORD
MALCOLM EPLEY
DONALD A. OHL
EDWARD A. KILLINGSWORTH
ROBERT WELLS
EDWARD LOVELL
D. W. CAMPBELL
PHIL HATTERY
NORBERT W. DEAN
DARRELL T. NEIGHBORS
MRS. RICHARD P. GLASGOW
WARREN D. HARPER
MRS. GEORGE P. TAUBMAN
ROBERT A. GRAHAM
JACKSON R. McGOWEN
GEORGE R. JOHNSON
GEORGE P. TAUBMAN
LAWRENCE A. COLLINS, SR.
DR. FRANCIS C. HERTZOG

December 4, 1964

ASSOCIATION OF WORLD WAR II
PILOTS AND AVIATION SPECIALISTS
Insurance Exchange Building
Long Beach, California

Gentlemen:

You can help build Long Beach into one of the world's famed beauty spots by supporting the plan to plant 3,000 flowering peach trees on our State College campus. Each spring, the campus will be transformed into a color spectacular rivaling the renowned cherry blossoms in our nation's capital.

A volunteer citizen's committee is working to raise the $15,000 necessary to buy and plant these flowering trees. Each tree costs $5.00. You can help in two ways: first, by securing a donation direct from your organization and, second, by acquainting your members and friends with the opportunity to make an individual gift of one or more trees.

We hope everyone in Long Beach will become a beauty-builder. The size of the gift is secondary in importance. DO NOT send gifts to our Committee but send them direct to the College where a special fund has been created in the tax deductible College Foundation. Checks should be made out and sent to:

Flowering Trees
California State College at Long Beach
6101 East Seventh Street
Long Beach, California 90804

A memorial of recognition with the names of all donors is planned for permanent display at the College. We hope your organization will add its name to this honor roll. If you have any questions, please contact us.

Sincerely,

Llewellyn Bixby, Jr.

Llewellyn Bixby, Jr.
Chairman

OUT

each tree

JOB NO. 66-2673

2 Feb.'66

News

Children contribute peach tree

VISIrecord Inc.,
Copiague, L. I., N.Y.
W 1985 / AP 10

AUDIO VISUAL - PHOTO REFERENCE RECORD
California State College at Long Beach

5 x 6 1."
#132
WLLCO. 4-11471

The campus community got behind the movement to plant fruit trees in the 1960s. The campaign brought lush greenery to what had been a rather stark campus.

An early campus shuttle. No one seemed to relish the hike from parking to classes on upper campus.

COLLEGE NAME EVOLVES WITH THE CAMPUS

1949: Los Angeles–Orange County State College

1950: Long Beach State College

1964: California State College at Long Beach

1968: California State College, Long Beach

1972: California State University, Long Beach

. . . Questions on financing

IS IT UNUSUAL TO VOTE ON A FEE? WHAT IS THE BASIC BENEFIT?

Yes. This is what the referendum is all about, required by the California State College Trustees. This is a really unusual opportunity. Few other colleges in the country give students the opportunity to understand or to decide on facilities for fees charged. Out of this experience, it becomes clear that fees for a college union building and operation are really an investment on the part of each student. For, in a given year's time, the return on this investment equals or exceeds the dollars paid in, in free services and lower cost entertainment and recreation. To say nothing of the enhancement of the students' prime purpose, education, which is supplemented by the learning that takes place through associations of students, with each other, and students with faculty outside of the classroom.

WHY MUST I HELP PAY FOR IT?

The California Educational Code clearly does not allow the construction of a College Union facility out of tax funds.

The only way we can get this facility is for we, the students, to provide it for ourselves. The College Union will add tremendously to campus life and to our individual gain from college. The graduated fee schedule is designed to make payment by current students, some of whom will enjoy its facilities only as alumni, as equitable as possible.

The wide range of facilities and activities planned for the Union will certainly provide something essential for everyone in the Union. And remember, too, that it is not all finally settled.

Your ideas for services, design, feeling, and atmosphere that you have not yet expressed, are readily welcomed and will help the development of the "details" of the interior planning.

VOTE!

When? March 22, 23, and 24

Where? Library, Cafeteria, Lower-Campus Cafeteria, and Little Theater

The College Union Committee, taking guidance from the survey and relying upon the experience of planners and its Advisory Group, proposes a project which takes advantage of the setting and climate.

. . . Lounges and reception room

After hours, the main lounge can easily be transformed to a reception room for teas and conventions. It will serve as the hospitality center for large functions such as the Homecoming Coronation ball, the Spring Prom, and Conventions.

Reception Room

Lounge

TV Lounge

The main lounge of the Union will be spacious and attractively decorated with massive chairs and couches, capable of accomodating many students who are looking for a place to relax. The lounge area will be the campus "living room;" the place to meet people, to discuss politics, to rest after a weary day.

Combination of the above facilities and the snack bar facility with their outdoor counterparts will provide a capacity of 3,000 seats at once.

. . . Snack bar

An additional and separate snack bar, designed with an informal atmosphere as focal point of student life, will serve as the food-coordinating center for the College Union. Informal entertainment, combos and other attractions will be offered, both at noon and during the evenings. Easily expandable, the snack bar will be able to serve large groups as well as the individual student.

Meeting Rooms

. . . Meeting and banquet rooms

Through the use of pneumatic walls, any combination of meeting rooms can be available for groups, either large or small. The Union will be able to accomodate groups numbering as large as 2,000 for national conventions of organizations on campus. Through functional design, the meeting facilities will definitely solve the problem "Where will our group meet?"

Banquet facilities for more than 1,500 persons will be available in the Union by transforming the meeting rooms into one large banquet hall. The banquet hall will also serve as a ballroom for such events as the Coronation Ball and the Spring Prom. Speakers-on-Campus may well take advantage of the spaciousness and accoustical engineering of the banquet room for their noon-time speeches.

Banquet Room

. . . Information and communication center

At the main entrance of the Union, the information center will accomodate most of the student's extra-curricular needs: an information counter, mutual ticket agency, telephones, lighted display cases and message marquee, post office services, banking facilities, bulletin boards, the Master Calendar of Events, and courteous students to answer all of your questions concerning events on campus.

Desk

Calendar

Chess

Pool

. . . Recreation facilities

Facilities will be provided for the student seeking something to do in his spare time . . . select from billiards, table tennis, bridge, chess, checkers, as well as outdoor games such as badminton, horseshoes, and miniature golf. In addition to the proposed recreation room, a swimming pool-barbecue patio area will greatly enhance group parties.

. . . Exhibit space

Sufficient space will be allowed for organizations and departments that wish to display projects and demonstrations. Display cabinets, lighted showcases, floor space, wall bulletin boards and tables for this purpose all will be an important part of our College Union.

Exhibit

Art Exhibit

. . . Cultural facilities

Music listening rooms, a small auditorium for recitals, and plays, art exhibit areas, and reading rooms will provide relaxation as well as study in a quiet atmosphere.

. . . Student services

The student-faculty committees which participated in the initial phases of planning quickly became aware of the needs for student services. Every conceivable service was brainstormed through committees and accepted or rejected as a feasible question to raise on the survey. The services now being planned represent the wants of a broad cross-section of the student body. These include:

Check rooms, telephones, files, work tables, lockers, resting and clean-up facilities; typing, duplicating, poster-making equipment; notary public, parking in designated parking lots at the edge of the union site, information center, lost and found, public address, luncheon and banquet service, TV viewing, tournaments, debates, movies, public forums, dances and programs of all kinds.

. . . Administration

Students
Faculty
Administration
Alumni

The College Union will be administered by a staff operating under policies developed by a representative student-faculty College Union Operating Board. The Board itself will be responsible to both the Associated Students and the Dean of Students. Membership on the College Union Board will be 8 students, 4 faculty members, 3 college officers, and 1 alumni member. The College Union Director is the ex-officio non-voting secretary.

The job of the College Union Board will be to develop policy for the operation of the College Union and to prepare and recommend the annual budget to the Associated Students and the Dean of Students, thus giving the students a stronger voice in the affairs of their College Union than in any other student-operated facility. In addition, the program in the Union will continue to be developed and administered by Associated Students' Commissions.

. . . Hours

Based upon the results of the questionnaire-survey, taken from a broad sampling of students, the following is the schedule of hours that the Union would be available.

Weekdays:	7 A.M. to 10 P.M. (Mon.-Thu.)
Friday:	7 A.M. to 12 Midnight
Saturday:	9 A.M. to 12 Midnight
Sunday:	9 A.M. to 10 P.M.

. . . The union is a substitute for:

no place to sit

no tables

the parked car

the isolation from the campus

the discontent with the same old pattern

the high school atmosphere

drudgery

. . . Commuter

For the commuter, the College Union provides the services of a home—a place to study, a place to sit between classes, a place to clean up.

A college union is one of the best investments a student can make:

in dollars (for he gets a full return on his investment)

in time (the rewards of discussion and committee work are lasting and essential know-how)

in use (yours for the using)

. . . Expected opening

If the schedule proceeds as now anticipated, the Union with the services described earlier, would be ready for full use in the Spring of 1968. Partial use of patio areas and other facilities will be made available when they reach completion.

. . . Decision

The decision on the CSC-LB Union will be made by Forty-Niner Students during the referendum to be held March 22, 23, and 24, 1965. A two-thirds majority of ballots cast is required to authorize the Union.

. . . Future planning

The proposed services and proposed facilities are subject to refinement and modification as our plans take form and details are considered: Also the College Union Committee and the personnel of the College Union Offices—LA 3-201—are eager to provide additional information and discuss the project and all ideas. So . . . ask, read, and above all, *vote*.

. . . Financing

The Union construction will cost an estimated $3,-280,000; furnishings and equipment will cost approximately $365,000, a total of $3,645,000. The required down payment on the structure of ten per cent ($328,000) is possible through savings of 49er Shops and the Cal-State Long Beach Foundation and initial student fees.

Operating costs will be covered through the fee schedule and net revenue from building services.

Cost of equipment and furnishings and preparatory expense will be covered by accumulation of funds prior to opening (first three years), this is necessary because the California State College System requires that we have in hand the necessary money for furnishings and equipment. We can provide this money only through the source of fees which will accumulate in sufficient amount, according to our schedule, until the opening of the building, from the proposed fee schedule:

	Fall '65	Spring '66	Fall '66	Spring '67	Fall '67	Spring '68	Fall '68	Spring '69	etc.
Full Time Students	None	None	3.00	3.00	8.00	8.00	8.00	8.00	etc.
Limited Students	None	None	1.50	1.50	4.00	4.00	4.00	4.00	etc.
Summer School	'66—None		'67—1.50		'68—4.00		'69—4.00		etc.

After opening, fee money will defray expense of operation and services to students. The cost above is entirely in keeping with the size of the College and what similar institutions are doing. The construction of the building, will be paid for by our obtaining a loan, probably from the Federal Government with the endorsement and support and authority of the State College Board of Trustees.

Student fees and net income from service facilities will repay the loan. The Federal Government is a low interest source of financing college service facilities. Part of the success of our program, in terms of schedule and completion, will be determined by the priority we obtain in getting our plans and programs completed and into the Federal Government.

The requirement of the State College System is that there be at least 10% of the construction costs in hand, in cash. This amount is being provided by the grant of the 49er Shops and Cal-State Long Beach Foundation, thus reducing the amount of the loan request and therefore the amount required for repayment by individual student fees. As stated earlier in discussing student's fees, the amount for movable equipment and furnishings which is not payable through a loan program, is furnished by the accumulation of students' fees during the months prior to the actual opening of the Union.

In summary the construction is financed by the amortization of a loan. The movable equipment and furnishings are paid for by student fees, accumulated.

Limited students will be given a full vote but will be assessed at approximately half the fee charged full-time students. Since the limited student group involves working and married students to a great extent, special efforts will be made to provide special services for them in the evening.

The 1969 groundbreaking for the University Student Union was the culmination of years of planning, including a 1965 referendum campaign to raise fees by eight dollars for full-time students.

1970s

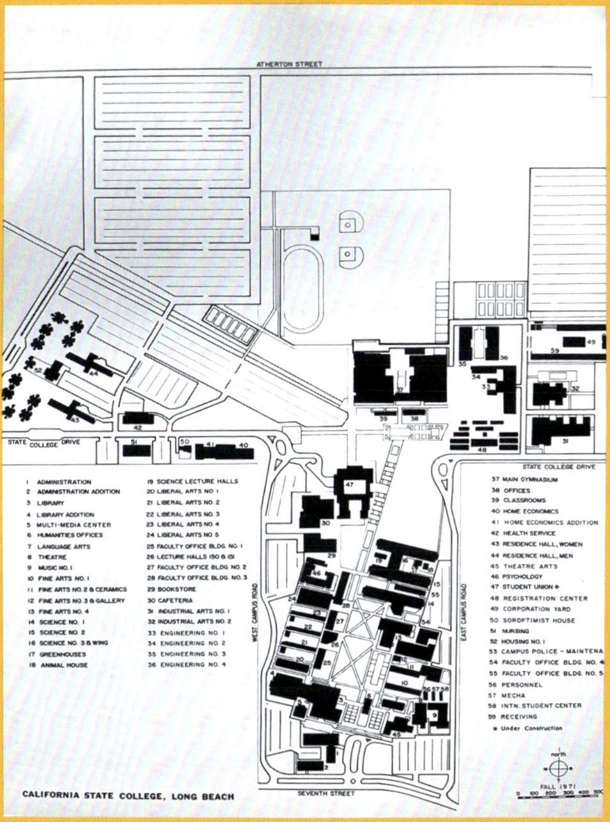

IN THIS 1971 CAMPUS MAP, the upper campus is starting to look like a college while lower campus to the north is still parking lot and scrub.

The two newish dorms—Los Alamitos and Los Cerritos—are on the left. In this late seventies photo, students wind 'round the bookstore aisles to purchase textbooks.

The Asian Scooper was a joint UCLA–Long Beach State publication that focused on the growing Asian communities of each college.

Students observe children and animals in these 1971 photos. The psychology department would eventually grow to become one of the biggest on campus.

Craig Stone

Craig Stone, a professor emeritus in American Indian Studies, came to Long Beach State in 1975 to do a presentation with an American Indian dance group. By 2023, Stone would be dancing for the third time as head man in the annual Pow Wow celebration that has grown to become the biggest American Indian gathering in LA and Orange County. He later worked with faculty to get ethnic studies requirements enshrined in California law. Long Beach State's American Indian Studies program is the oldest and one of the largest in the CSU system.

"

I came to Cal State Long Beach because it was known as a good American Indian school. I met my wife the first week ... She came here because it was a good Japanese American school. It was written about in the *Rafu Shimpo* and the *Nichi Bei Times*.

When I showed up on campus, I had this beaded belt buckle that said Craig Stone on it. I went up to the [American Indian Studies] office, and they said can we help you? And they said, nice belt buckle. Where'd you get it? I said, I made it. They said, are you Craig Stone? ... They said, we know all about you! Welcome! So that was my first day on campus. That's called community recognition. It was such a good feeling to be welcomed in that way.

LAWRENCE FORTENBERRY

"THERE WERE FRIENDSHIPS TO BE MADE"

Los Angeles native Lawrence Fortenberry remembers Long Beach State as a "city within a city," which seemed overwhelming at first. He didn't see many Black students, but he found the Black Student Union and knew "there were friendships to be made."

Fortenberry joined the BSU right away and heard speakers such as Angela Davis in a little room near Lecture Hall 150. He didn't believe then-President Steve Horn was listening to Black students' demands. At 23, and older than most students, Fortenberry enrolled in the Educational Opportunity Program created to help low-income and first-generation students. A language arts teacher suggested Fortenberry write about the BSU meetings.

"When I wrote about them, she told me, 'You have some journalistic touches here; why don't you go to the journalism department?' I was married at the time, and my wife went with me. We couldn't afford books, and we met with Dr. Ben Cunningham, the *Forty-Niner* advisor. When we left, our arms were full of books." At the time, the BSU was complaining about the *Forty-Niner's* coverage, and "that's one reason he was so welcoming."

Fortenberry found the journalism professors helpful, and when he started writing for the *Forty-Niner*, he discovered a calling as a journalist. After graduating, he went on to work for the *Los Angeles Sentinel*, *Muhammad Speaks*, as well as the *Wave* local newspapers. He also performed stand-up comedy in area clubs, including The Comedy Store in West Hollywood. He believes journalism helped with comedy because he understood his writing had to be succinct to be funny. He retired from the City of Long Beach after twenty-five years of working in the city's Section 8 housing program.

Fortenberry saw his time on campus and working for the newspaper as "one of the highlights of my life. I look back fondly on it to this day because it opened up so many things to me."

TIM GROBATY

"A PRETTY HIP PLACE TO BE"

Longtime Long Beach reporter and columnist Tim Grobaty was on campus as a Long Beach State student "for a cup of coffee" before eventually dropping out. But he enjoyed a much longer history as a neighborhood kid, running on campus and getting to hear famous bands of the day.

"My friend and I scampered across the street," he recalled, where they saw Chicago Transit Authority (later Chicago) playing with Spirit and Jefferson Airplane in 1968 when he was twelve years old. They played on the hillside . . . Spirit had a hit: "I Got a Line on You." Jefferson Airplane played "White Rabbit." "A hell of a show," Grobaty said.

He recalled going behind the art buildings and pulling sculptures out of the trash, running around, and trying to avoid the police. He remembered students in the TV room watching *Dark Shadows*. He also recalled an expansive campus of open hillsides and tumbleweeds occasionally rolling down Palos Verdes Drive.

"By the time I enrolled there I was already tired of the place," Grobaty said. "I pretty much knew it like the back of my hand. My friends and I were there all the time. We'd play football on the field and play pinball in the student union. You could buy cigarettes there out of the machines, and they had *Rolling Stone* in the news racks. It was a pretty hip place to be."

Grobaty got a job as a copyboy at the *Press-Telegram* in the 1970s, and he gave up on his higher education. As a reporter, however, he met and interviewed many of the college founders, including famed architect Ed Killingsworth, who shared an interesting fact: "The campus planners left the upper campus open to see what paths students would follow. 'Desirelines,' they called them."

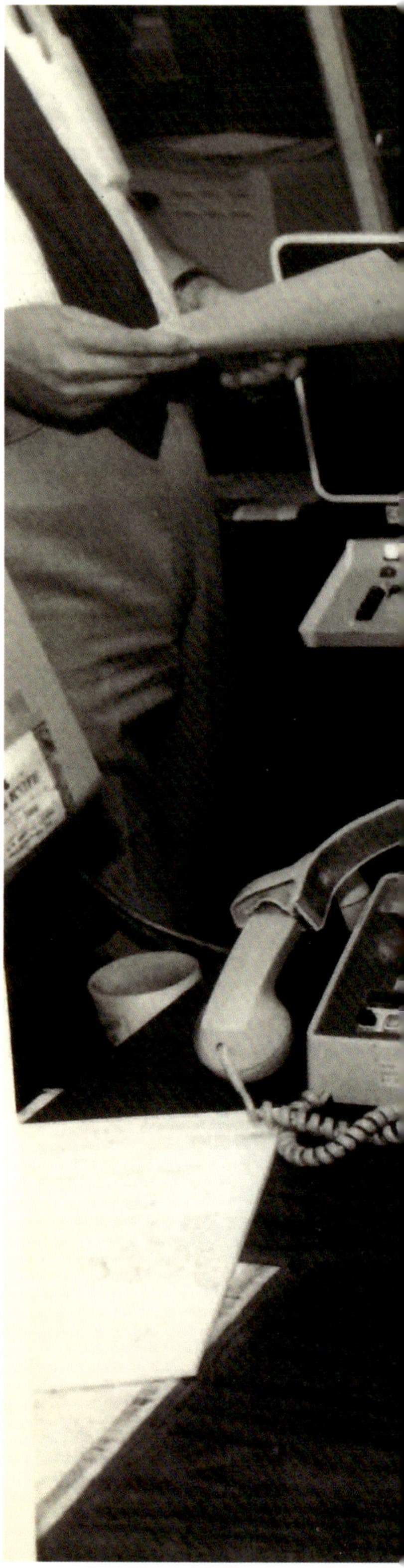

Columnist Tim Grobaty, a longtime CSULB campus neighbor, in the *Press-Telegram* newsroom in 1980.

Ed Killingsworth (left) was the famed Case Study Homes architect whose firm was hired in the 1960s to shape the growing campus's master plan. The hiring marked a bureaucratic shift that took planning away from the Sacramento-based architect and allowed a local independent firm more creative control. The result was less concrete, more brick, and more flourishes, including the dappled-light walking spaces outside the USU. Killingsworth, pictured with Dean of Development Frances "Frenchy" Flynn and landscape architect Ed Lovell (right) helped launch the peach tree campaign to beautify the campus in 1965. The three are planting Helen Borchers peach trees, the first of many campaigns to plant and replace older trees to keep the campus green. Killingsworth would stay involved in campus planning until his retirement in 2001.

Roy Nakano

When Roy Nakano transferred from Cal State Los Angeles to LBSU in 1972, he found a dynamic campus with an established Asian American studies program and Asian Student Center.

"

The first time I set foot on the Long Beach campus left a lasting impression. I had just transferred from another state university, but the vibes were so different. The school I left was modern to the point of being sterile, and the students rarely stuck around the campus after class. In contrast, the grassy Long Beach campus in 1972 was not quite as modern-looking, but students stayed on the campus after class—or at least stuck around the surrounding community. That the campus was situated near a beach was surely a contributing factor.

This may explain in part why the campus activities were so lively. Of course, the early 1970s were also a time for student activism all over the country. At Long Beach, the two factors combined to make it an ideal venue for learning both inside and outside the classrooms.

When I first registered for classes at Cal State Long Beach, the friendly clerk at the counter said, 'Your English is very good. How long have you been in the States?'

'This is my second state college,' I replied, thinking she was referring to the California state college system. It didn't dawn on me until later she assumed I was a foreigner and not the third-generation American I am.

That micro-distraction aside, Cal State Long Beach felt welcoming. The weather, grassy lawns and active student body all played a part. Older alumni shared stories about the lack of diversity during the 1950s and sixties. By the early 1970s, however, Long Beach was quite diverse. Ethnic studies courses were part of the curriculum for the first time. I took courses that covered the experiences of my family as part of the American experience. I was able to minor in Asian American Studies.

Later that year, I served as the student representative for a hiring committee to select the new dean of Student Development Programs, overseeing EOP, Upward Bound, and a number of other campus programs. We ended up hiring Alan Nishio, who is now a lifelong friend. Alan has had a massive impact on the Long Beach campus, not to mention the Japanese American and Asian American communities. Alan went on to play a key role in the movement to secure redress for the Japanese Americans who were placed in US incarceration camps during the 1940s.

When I transferred to Cal State Long Beach in 1972, Asian American Studies and the Asian American Student Center were already up and running.

. . . the Asian American Student Association was in full swing. The first Asian American Week was planned for the campus. An Asian women's rap group met regularly. There was an Asian American veterans group called Asian Americans for Military Outreach. The Pilipino American Coalition was launched at that time. The Union of Vietnamese Students were active. There was a Cal State Long Beach publication called *Yellow Journalism*, which merged with efforts from UCLA to publish a joint student journal [the *Scooper*].

Many of the pioneers from that era have sadly passed away. I do know, however, that Dan Kuramoto was the first person to teach Asian American Studies at Cal State Long Beach. Dan later went on to form the Asian American jazz group Hiroshima.

THE CAMPUS

- The Long Beach State campus is like an upside-down T. And the main part (with limited parking) is crowded in the skinny stem to the south. To the north are athletic fields, the Student Recreation and Wellness Center, dorms, Puvungna, Carpenter Center, and the rest.
- For years the northern part of campus consisted of a few physical education buildings—the temporary buildings used before the permanent buildings were finished. Officials in the early days couldn't imagine needing all that space to the north, and stuck to that idea, even when students were pouring in during the 1960s, when the campus was ballooning from 10,000 in 1960 to 26,000 in 1970.
- When Long Beach State started with a few hundred, then a few thousand, students and 322 acres, there was still plenty of extra space. (Cal State Fullerton, for instance, has 236 acres. The University of Southern California, 226.) First President P. Victor Peterson revealed years later that he and campus officials would spitball about what to do with the northern part of campus. Agriculture? Farming? Parking? Sports? For a while they used much of it for parking and recreation, and the rest to the sheep and the rabbits.
- As the student population exploded beyond anyone's imagination, planners were forced to regroup. But the library and all the main buildings stayed at one edge of the campus, with parking, engineering, and PE down below. The 1962 master plan noted it was essentially too late to do anything about it.

- Campus planners tried to make it work. But when new President Stephen Horn, in 1970, saw plans to build another liberal arts building in the central quad, which was finally getting a little more attractive with trees and sculptures, he put his foot down and demanded it be moved.
- The Social Science/Public Affairs building went to lower campus instead—in a flood plain, with a basement, which led to its own problems. Horn did the same thing with the Administration building, and Brotman Hall now occupies the old dusty open space that was once used for the 49er Days celebration.

An unfolding scene of creative action . . .a panorama

Shed the boundaries of a young college, and gradually, yet inevitably, a great institution emerges - - a center of creativity. Add a building, a new course, and a new major . . . Put in a dash of fresh ideas . . . Flavor it with a broadened graduate program . . . Mix the influx of new students with new personnel.

Behold, a panorama!

“It was a nice campus, but it had a tremendous hill. You’d park on lower campus where they had bungalows, and you had that darn hill—120 or whatever steps to get to the top. A block long of steps. All you had on lower campus was the recreation department, women’s and men’s PE parking lots, and the police station up top by the Administration building. We ended up having all our academic buildings on top of the hill. You had to go up the hill to go anywhere.”

—LAURA (MURPHY) TERRY, 1971 graduate

“My first impression of the campus was that there had been a lot of money spent to create a deliberate impression of economy without the reality of it. There were some buildings here which were almost deliberately made to look ugly, so they would look cheap. Despite this, it had all the potential for a beautiful campus.”

—CARL MCINTOSH, LBSU President, 1959–1969

“When it rained, it was a god-awful mess. One free lot was all dirt. And when it rained, it was just incredible. The tow trucks and winches would come out. When students came out [to get their cars] they had mud up to here on their shoes, ankle deep.”

—LEE BROWN, 1960 LBSU graduate

THE TARKANIAN YEARS AND THE GOLD MINE GYM

Former 49er coach Jerry Tarkanian and three of his very best: left to right, Chuck Terry, Ed Ratleff, and George Trapp

Glenn McDonald hit that sweet spot between two coaching legends. He played for Coach Jerry Tarkanian from 1971–73 and then one year for future Basketball Hall of Famer Lute Olson. McDonald would help lead the 49ers to a national No. 2 ranking and back-to-back Elite Eight appearances in the NCAA tournament. He joined a talented team that included guard Ed Ratleff, who was one of the Americans to refuse silver medals when the Soviets won a controversial Olympic basketball final in 1972. Ratleff would be inducted into the College Basketball Hall of Fame in 2015, after playing for the Houston Rockets. McDonald would make a key playoff appearance to help the 1976 Boston Celtics beat the Phoenix Suns and eventually win their thirteenth NBA title.

McDonald, raised along with his three sisters by a single mother in South Central LA, always liked the idea of playing for an underdog. Tarkanian promised him that unheralded Long Beach State could compete with schools like UCLA, which was in the midst of its march to ten NCAA titles in twelve years. McDonald actually liked the fact that Long Beach played its games in the tiny, hot, 2,400-seat Gold Mine Gym.

And hot it was. Fans crammed inside the building, which was built in 1958, and screamed their heads off. When that wasn't loud enough, they banged wood blocks together. As the fan count and decibel level rose, the walls would literally sweat. Moisture would run down the sides of the beige building walls just behind the pull-out wooden bleachers.

"It was hotter than hot, louder than loud," remembered former student and later college administrator Gary Little. "It was fun, but you'd come out of there needing a shower."

Fans were loud and fierce. For the NCAA tournament, the students had prepared a cheer for UCLA's Bill Walton, the red-haired, seven-foot star center: "Walton, Walton, don't be blue, Frankenstein was ugly, too!" Big games were moved to the Long Beach Arena. In 1973, the 49ers beat an Al McGuire–led Marquette team 76–66 in front of almost 12,000 screaming fans. Two years before, Long Beach State came within three points of beating UCLA in the NCAA West Regional final at the apex of the John Wooden era.

The Gold Mine became a regular old gym when the $22 million Walter Pyramid went up in 1994. But the gym, PE site, and summer gathering spot for 49ers camp youth found itself back in the spotlight in 2023 when the women's basketball team and men's volleyball team were forced to hold games there due to Walter Pyramid leaks.

STEPHEN HORN

John Stephen "Steve" Horn helped Long Beach State grow from a small college to a larger university with a stronger focus on research. He stared down student protesters and battled with coaches and faculty alike.

"He professionalized the university," said former College of Liberal Arts dean and History chair Dee Abrahamse. "But he had a difficult personality."

Born in Gilroy, in 1931, and raised in San Juan Bautista, the family wasn't poor but lived a country life. There was no electricity in the home until Stephen was ten, and no telephone until he was a high school senior. Young Horn climbed oil rigs that were rising up in the farming community in the 1940s. His keen interest in government would bookend his time as Long Beach State president, from 1970 to 1988.

He interned for the US secretary of labor and a US senator in the years before he came to Long Beach State and was a Republican US congressman after he left the college. He was also vice chairman of the US Civil Rights Commission.

At the university, Horn had plenty to say about a lot of things, and sometimes he would follow with decisive—some faculty would say dictatorial—action.

In 1973, he fired winning basketball coach Jerry Tarkanian after an internal investigation, and later the NCAA found recruiting violations and special treatment for players. Tarkanian, of course, went on to big success at the University of Nevada, Las Vegas, where he won a national championship.

Horn's interest in cleaning up the program—he said he previously had little need for sports, or exercise, for that matter—came after a chance dinner conversation with legendary UCLA basketball coach John Wooden. The coach said that Long Beach State was not part of the national letter of intent, and he asserted that Long Beach State was, in effect, stealing other teams' players.

Horn said later Wooden called LBSU a "bandit operation." This raised Horn's hackles and prompted the president to take an interest in athletics and, eventually, the powerful National Collegiate Athletic Association.

Horn started attending NCAA meetings in the Midwest—one of the first university presidents to do so. The NCAA members were tickled at first.

Then in the mid-1970s, Horn proposed NCAA member schools share TV revenue with the poorer schools, including his own. He was labeled "Robin Hood." USC's John McKay seethed, saying Horn's plan amounted to "communism," and asked, according to the *Independent Press-Telegram*, "Where did he come from anyway?"

Horn, meanwhile, had been launching a letter-writing campaign to get all member presidents involved in the NCAA, and it worked. To make a very long story short, TV revenue was shared among conference members and, to an extent, within the NCAA. "All those things he promoted came to pass," said Perry Moore, the former LBSU athletic director hired by Horn. But at the time, "they thought he was nuts."

On campus, Horn instituted classroom evaluations, and alumni fundraising became professional instead of the shoebox operation it had been. Changes in alumni affairs started in 1970, prompting the *Forty-Niner* headline "CSULB Starts Keeping Records of Alumni after 20 Years of Not Doing It."

Horn also tried to address the long-standing problem of chilly town/gown relations. *Press-Telegram* columnist Hank Hollingsworth coined the term "Mausoleum on the Hill" in the 1960s to refer to a lack of school spirit on campus. The term was also taken to reflect the campus's lack of community involvement. Horn responded by championing low-cost senior education, and he and his wife, Nini Horn, started to work with donors to generate institutions that would serve the community and not just the students—those included the Isabel Patterson Child Development Center and the Richard and Karen Carpenter Performing Arts Center.

Meanwhile, Horn clashed repeatedly with faculty, who found him arrogant and unwilling to listen to them and prone to act unilaterally. Faculty censured him twice. Emeritus History Professor David Bernstein said Horn seemed hostile toward the tenure system while other faculty complained he made them vulnerable to layoffs in the early eighties when the university faced steep budget cuts.

Battles with faculty were taking their toll, and when he locked horns with Cal State Chancellor W. Ann Reynolds, it was the beginning of the end. Horn resigned in 1988 and stayed to teach a political science class.

Steve Horn and former student and philanthropist Isabel Patterson with a model of the Child Development Center.

Politics and his strong personality may have ended his academic career, but he wasn't finished. Horn ran for congress in 1988, losing to conservative Republican and 1969 Long Beach State grad Dana Rohrabacher. But Horn ran for a newly apportioned 38th Congressional District in 1992 and won as a moderate Republican. He stayed for ten years until another reapportionment by Democrats tilted his district to their party.

Mark Mayuga, a 1969 graduate who later worked at the university and was family friends with Horn, said Horn "had a vision of what Cal State Long Beach was and what the standards should be . . . He tried to hold professors to a higher standard."

Horn retired in 2001 and died ten years later. The university staged a celebration of his life, complete with testimonials describing the changes he made to Long Beach State during his seventeen-and-a-half years as university president.

ISABEL PATTERSON

"THOSE WHO ARE ABLE TO SHARE SHOULD SHARE"

(Opposite page) Isabel Patterson with children at the 1975 opening of the child development center that bears her name.

Isabel Patterson was the eighteenth student to register at the new college. She had served in World War II. When she read a small item in the paper about a new college opening, she paid a nickel to ride the bus and registered at the new Long Beach college for $12.50. She was one of the first editors of the *Forty-Niner* newspaper and helped pick the mascot colors (brown and gold, later changed to black and gold) and the 49er mascot. She later became a second-grade teacher, successful Realtor, and philanthropist. She was blunt-spoken, talkative, and honest, according to several news accounts. Two of her favorite subjects included Long Beach State and what she considered an essential duty to give back to the community.

"Almost everything I do is geared toward children and education," Patterson once said, according to a 1996 *Press-Telegram* article. "I really believe—and I step on toes by saying this—that those who are able to share should share."

In the 1970s and eighties, she gave millions in scholarships to Long Beach City College and Long Beach State students, the university, the city, her First Congregational Church in downtown Long Beach, as well as the Child Development Center that bears her name. She died in 1996 and left no will, having steadily given away her fortune over the years. Her few belongings were auctioned off to pay for supplies for the CDC.

"

> So I have to tell you, I had some friends here playing bridge. And they're all showing off their jewelry, which I have very little . . . And so, how much they paid for

> this and all that; couldn't resist buying this diamond ring. So I got up and left the table. I went in and put on a T-shirt that I'd gotten from City College kids. And this has got little hearts on here and says, "We love Isabel," it says "We (heart) Isabel." And I said, "Here's my jewelry." I said, "Eleven hundred scholarships were given there this year. Eleven hundred scholarships, $1,500 apiece, to keep kids in school."
>
> I get many, many letters from the students that say they couldn't go to school if it weren't for that. One day I was in Penney's, and I wanted to write a check. And the clerk looked at my check and she looked at me and she says, "Are you Isabel Patterson?" she said. "Are you *the* Isabel Patterson?" And I said, "Well, I'm Isabel." And she said, "My child goes to your school." She said she couldn't work otherwise and was just happy to have it. "It's just such a good place."

She gave more than $800,000 to create the Child Development Center, located on Atherton Street:

> I looked over there and saw that. I'd seen it many times before. But this time I looked and I thought, "That's my monument." I don't need a big tombstone in a cemetery. Right there's my monument. Ever since then I've been very proud and I love it.
>
> **—FROM A 1987 INTERVIEW**

WOMEN'S ATHLETICS—ALWAYS READY TO PLAY

Dorothy Deatherage helped shape a fledgling intercollegiate athletics program at Long Beach State.

When it came to women's sports, Long Beach State was always ready to play—and not just on the field. The young college had strong administrators determined to fight for money for its physical education program and, eventually, gym time for a nascent women's intercollegiate program.

Female administrators "were responsible for building a really strong women's program before Title IX," said Gary Little, an LBSU athlete and student body president in the sixties. "And they were forceful women."

They had their work cut out for them. A history of the college's first ten years showed that by 1959 the college could boast "a full program of intercollegiate athletics" of eleven sports, none of which accommodated women. Resources weren't the only problem.

"Those of you in this generation cannot conceive of what it was like for a woman with athletic talent," former basketball and volleyball coach Fran Schaafsma told the *Daily Forty-Niner* in 1983. "I'm talking about the fifties . . . . The cultural stigma was that if you wanted to be an athlete, your femininity was somehow suspect."

They used a combination of personality and perseverance to build a program.

Soft-spoken, golf-loving Dorothy Deatherage was hired away from her job teaching PE at Wilson High to join a staff of determined female administrators. Deatherage originally rejected the idea of joining her local college after she learned the fledgling PE department stored its equipment in a bathtub. But she was encouraged by C. Patricia Reid, then a PE instructor in charge of recruiting new teachers. A meeting with President P. Victor Peterson and a golf game with the head of the college's physical education department helped convince Deatherage to come to Long Beach State.

Reid later became chair of the women's physical education department. The women had to overcome some apathy on campus and, like everyone else, a notable lack of facilities. Women practiced dancing and gymnastics on a dirt lot. They used the plunge at the Long Beach Pike for swimming. A petite woman, Reid was friendly, personable, and easy to get along with. And she was never afraid to stand up for women's physical education and, eventually, women's athletics.

When the first gym opened in the mid-1950s, the men took it over, and the women pretty much played sports outside. But when the "big, beautiful men's gym," often called the West Gym, was finished in 1958, the women got the old East Gym. The men still wanted to use that gym as well for basketball and other sports. And they had to ask Reid, who told them, "Sorry, that gym is reserved for ladies' sports." That response, she recalled later, "was not too well received."

"The program wasn't very big and wasn't very good," Reid said later, "but we had a program, and we were going to develop it." When women's intercollegiate sports were starting out in 1960s, Reid "spent a good amount of time convincing the president that it would boost the whole program to hire women and not just another male coach."

Deatherage took over women's intercollegiate athletics in 1964 with a budget of $400. "There was no Title IX, no nothing. We would each year make our appeal to the ASI board of control . . . Nobody cared in those days . . . But every year we made our pitch, and our money would grow."

The women's volleyball team started winning in the 1960s and 1970s under coach Dixie Grimmett, who won two national championships in the early 1970s under the old Association for Intercollegiate Athletics for Women. But nobody cared then, either, or so it seemed, according to Grimmett.

"Back when I called Long Beach newspapers to report our win and the names of the girls who had won, I was told, 'They didn't think they had room in the newspaper for us; it wasn't very newsworthy.' Not many people followed volleyball at that point," Grimmett told the *Daily Forty-Niner* in 2023.

Joan Bonvicini and star guard LaTaunya Pollard, who captured the Wade Trophy as college basketball's top woman player. Bonvicini led the team to ten NCAA tournament and two Final Four appearances.

Then the basketball team started building a following under Schaafsma, who compiled a 208–73 record. (Schaafsma also, for a time, coached volleyball and basketball at the same time, and both to lopsided winning records.)

Fans and media started paying more attention when Joan Bonvicini started coaching the women's team in 1979. She stayed until 1991 before moving on to the University of Arizona and Seattle University.

She was known for her brash style. When teams complained she was running up the score, she told them to find better players. When the Russian women's team came to town for a series of exhibition games in the 1980s, the 49ers beat them on a late basket. The Russians had beaten Los Angeles area teams by thirty points.

The Russian coach groused about the game immediately after, saying if the teams played tomorrow, the Russian team would win easily. That's when Bonvicini answered: "The problem is we're not playing them tomorrow. That's why we beat them today."

The Long Beach women's basketball team made it to the Final Four in 1987 and 1988 under teams led by guard Penny Toler, a transfer from San Diego State who would go on to become executive vice president and general manager of the Los Angeles Sparks. Toler said the intensely competitive Bonvicini encouraged players to be creative on the court and was just fun to play for.

"She was funny, and she had a great personality," Toler said. "The thing that was always her secret weapon is that she was warm. She was one hell of recruiter and had the gift of gab. Here was this white lady going into the inner city to recruit the best basketball players, players who could go to USC and UCLA. They had the Sports Arena and the Wooden Center, and we had this tiny gym, and she had the top five kids coming out of high school . . . NC State and Louisiana Tech—here comes Joan . . . She was warm and likable and that's how she got the recruits."

Penny Toler was a Long Beach State star who went on to play for the Los Angeles Sparks. She became general manager, and led the team to two WNBA championships.

Long Beach Blues Festival

1980s

THE 1980S BROUGHT FURTHER GROWTH IN CAMPUS ORGANIZATIONS, campus facilities, campus controversy, and even campus cats. Men's basketball and women's volleyball would take off while football rolled on for a few more years.

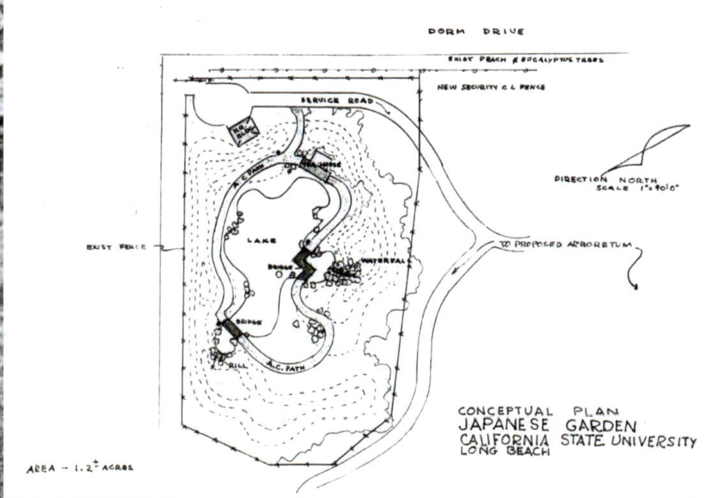

Earl B. Miller Japanese Garden opens in 1981 with a bridge, koi pond, bamboo, and bonsai to provide "a place of refuge, beauty and learning for all who enter its gates."

CSULB History – Campus Cats

Sept. 18, 1984

CAMPUS CATS CAMPUS CATS CAMPUS CATS CAMPUS CATS

The number of wild and abandoned cats on campus has reached the stage that Plant Operations has been forced to address the problem directly. They were advised by a humane organization that the only solution was euthanasia for all the cats. Their feeling is that no one has provided any other comprehensive alternative all these years and is not likely to now.

However, for years some of us have scooped up newly dumped cats and kittens, had them neutered and found them homes. Others have provided as much food on campus as their budgets would allow. I have a long standing interest in animal rights and animal communication. The problem of animal displacement and abandonment as society becomes increasingly urbanized is monumental. Although there are many organizations addressing this problem, they hardly make a dent. I would like to establish a "center" or "league" on the campus to first deal with the problem in our own back yard and further to provide a base for research, education, and community outreach.

As regards the immediate issue, the campus cats: I have a vet who will advise on controls and who will provide neutering and shots at greatly reduced rates. I will provide organizational services, solicit outside funding for help with the cats here and to establish an educational program, and pursue tax exempt status. Plant Operations will listen to our proposal. But it is all for naught unless you help. Please fill out the form below and return it to me, Sandy McMillan, Dept. of Radio-TV-Film, UTC 208, as soon as possible. Please attend an organizational meeting: Friday, September 21, noon until two, LA 2-100.

Name:______________________ Dept.______________ Ext.________

Please check generously all that apply.

1. I pledge $5____ $10____ $20____ per month for food, parasite control and vet care.
2. I pledge $20____ $40____ more $______ for initial neutering and shots fund.
3. I pledge approximately 2____ 4____ more ____ hours per week to distribute food, clean up wastes, monitor for illness and newly dumped cats, and provide TLC.
4. I am interested in working with a community education program concerning neutering, abandonment, public health, animal rights, and animal communication. Yes____ No____
5. I have special knowledge in animal care, rights, and/or communication. Yes____ No____

Not printed at State expense.

The cat population grows as legions of volunteers continue to feed them. The trend would extend into the 2000s until campus officials, concerned they were attracting coyotes, finally had them removed.

Daily Forty-Niner

California State University, Long Beach | Tuesday, May 11, 1982 | Vol. XXXIII, No. 142

Instructors say academic rights in danger

Staff Photo by Aurelio Jose Barrera

SPACE INVADER — Mary Jane Mailander attracts attention as she walks through campus Monday in a spacesuit as part of U.S. space program day at the Speakers Platform.

Probes allegedly directed at content of three courses

By Silvia da Costa
Staff Writer

Inquiries into the course content of at least three Cal State Long Beach classes has caused concern among some instructors that their academic freedom may be in danger.

While the origins and details of the probes is still to some degree unclear, teachers have tied three state legislators and a local church to the investigations.

At issue are:

—Non-students attempting to sit in classes to evaluate course content;

—Criticisms of the liberal content of some courses;

—The activities of the Grace Brethern Church of Long Beach (linked to the issue by several instructors at CSULB);

—The involvement of state senator H.L. Richardson.

—CSULB President Stephen Horn asking those involved not to make the matter public and refusing to comment on the investigations.

The probe, launched by off-campus sources, is looking into Women's Studies 101 "Women and Their Bodies," Psychology 457, "Psychology of Sex," and Comparative Literature 450, "Literature of Peace and War."

The probe into the Women's Studies class, taught by Betty Brooks and Gale Goldstein, is being conducted at the request of Jessica Shaver, who sent a letter to members of the state Senate and to the Grace Brethern Church.

Shaver's involvement is itself a mystery.

She claims she is a student at CSULB, but she refused to comment any further on the subject because she has promised Horn she would not make the issue public.

It has been learned, however, that Shaver has never

Please See CLASS, Page 7

CURRICULUM MATTERS/ WOMEN'S STUDIES

Women's studies were introduced at Long Beach State in the 1970s, springing forth from a meeting of women on campus. Courses included women's history and literature, and also "Women and Their Bodies," a basic course on women's health and women's sexuality.

In the seventies at CSULB, being a lesbian, or talking about it, was "very controversial, and anything to do with women's sexuality was considered radical and frightening," said Dee Abrahamse, a professor who was part of the history department then. Betty Brooks, a strong community activist and out lesbian, taught courses in the early 1980s on women's sexuality and violence against women, and gave presentations on self-examination, using slides.

The Women's Studies program and the Women's Center on campus came under attack in 1982 from members of a local church; the California chair of Phyllis Schlafly's Eagle Forum; and members of the state Legislature, according to a 1968–1976 history of the department by Julie Bartolotto, who would later go on to lead the Historical Society of Long Beach. The group went to President Steve Horn and attacked women's studies for not teaching "traditional American values" and allegedly interjecting a lesbian emphasis in "Women and Their Bodies."

The ACLU got involved and sued after two faculty members were fired and the Women's Center had closed. The case drew widespread attention, and the ousted instructors won a settlement. The lawsuit halted the erosion of the department; by the 2000s, the campus would have a Women's & Gender Equity Center, and by 2023 the department of Women's, Gender and Sexuality Studies would offer a BA and thirty-one courses in its catalog.

SETH GREENBERG

"YOU'LL NEVER WIN"

When newly hired LBSU men's assistant basketball coach Seth Greenberg showed up at Long Beach State in 1987, he was told he would never win and that he and head coach Joe Harrington should keep their bags packed.

The team's home court was a "PE gym," cavernous, Greenberg recalls, with lines on the floor for badminton and volleyball.

"When I thought of Long Beach State, I thought of Jerry Tarkanian. I thought of [Olympian] Ed Ratleff. I thought of, you know, the great tradition. But I didn't realize that . . . they'd moved out of the Long Beach Arena and that they're playing in this little high school gym," which was showing its age by the 1980s.

Greenberg, who would later become an NCAA analyst for ESPN, would help rebrand the old gym as The Gold Mine, and a loud, tough home court.

The team moved into the brand-new $23 million Pyramid (later the Walter Pyramid). As head coach, Greenberg compiled a 105–70 record from 1990–1996, ushering in one of the most dynamic eras of play.

The aggressive, up-tempo style turned games into a sweaty and exhilarating experience for fans inside and outside of the venue.

"When we were good, it was like there were six people on the court," said Greenberg. "And it was a huge, huge advantage. And then we went out and we did three-on-three tournaments in the middle of campus, and we went out and met community members and got them excited about what we were gonna do. We were very, very visible in the community."

(Opposite page) Seth Greenberg with future NBA player James Cotton. Greenberg celebrates with players after winning the Big West in 1995.

Greenberg's winning percentage was second only to Jerry Tarkanian at Long Beach State, and he led the team to the NCAA tournament twice and a Big West Conference championship in 1996.

Greenberg went on to the University of South Florida and Virginia Tech, then ESPN.

"I regret leaving. It was a great community. I love Dr. [Robert] Maxson and he was great to me . . . You know, obviously I took another job for another challenge . . . I survived South Florida, had great success coaching the ACC, and I'm going on an eleven-year career for ESPN. It's one of those moves that you look back and say you know what could have been. We could have been Gonzaga before Gonzaga was Gonzaga."

Dirtbags Coach Dave Snow

The Long Beach State baseball team was coming off several losing seasons when coach Dave Snow took over in 1989. The team didn't have a consistent baseball field for games, and they often practiced in the all-dirt pony league field at Whaley Park.

> "
>
> The field on campus was in really rough shape. It was not what you would call a college field. Part of the thing about going over there [to the Whaley Park pony league field] was to develop some mental toughness and take ground balls on an all-dirt field. [Assistant coach] Dave Malpass, one day he brought those guys back from a workout sweating dirt from top to bottom, and made the comment, "you guys look like a bunch of dirtbags" and that's kinda what we are. Those guys took on that mantra. That team went on to the NCAA record that year. The year before, in 1988, they won fourteen games and in 1989, the team won fifty [going to the College World Series]. It's still a record as far as I know. People always ask me about that year.

The football team, pictured in 1988, won a PCAA Championship in 1981. But the team often struggled to draw fans. And there were still outlets for that old college spirit.

STEVE MARTIN

"I'M GOING TO PLAY ALL THE TOILETS IN THE COUNTRY"

Comedian and actor Steve Martin studied philosophy for three years at Long Beach State before he transferred to UCLA to study theater. Martin didn't graduate from either institution, but in 1989, Long Beach State handed Martin its first honorary doctorate—in humanities. During the August ceremony, the comedian known for his movies, stand-up act, and *Saturday Night Live* King Tut number, mused about which one of his esteemed comedic works earned him his honorary degree.

Wearing a black cap and gown and doctoral hood, Martin recited his lyrics from the famous number, ending "Born in Arizona, moved to Babylonia/Born in Arizona, got a condo made of stone-a, King Tut."

Next he recited poetry from his film *The Man with Two Brains*:

"Pointy birds, oh pointy pointy.
Anoint my head, anointy-nointy."

Then he turned to newly inaugurated President Curtis McCray, who held a doctorate in English, and remarked, "I'm sure you're sorry you took up Chaucer now."

Martin's banjo-playing won him the Sigma Pi Hootenanny at Long Beach State in 1964. He broke into television in 1966, when a friend recommended him to Stu Rosen, a recent Long Beach State film grad who was producing a children's TV show in LA called *Dusty's Attic*. Rosen, who would go on to win several daytime Emmys, needed a banjo player, and a mutual friend recommended Martin, who was working on his magic act at Knott's Berry Farm.

Steve Martin cracks up new president Curtis McCray.

They met at Rosen's parents' house in Park Estates. Rosen recalled that Martin showed up for the first shoot with a fever. But he did the show. "He was funny. He was great," Rosen said.

Martin went on to write for *The Smothers Brothers* TV show. The next time Rosen spoke with Martin, in the mid-1970s, Martin told him, "I'm not going to write anymore, I'm going to go on the road for myself and I'm going to play all the toilets in the country" to get experience. And that's what Martin did.

Former Gov. Brown speaks at CSULB — Page 5

School of Business is accredited — Page 7

49er baseball team pounds UCI — Page 12

DAILY FORTY-NINER

California State University, Long Beach | Vol. XLII, No. 106 | Tuesday, April 23, 1

CSULB to freeze admissions

Budget constraints mean fewer students

By Danielle Jullen
Daily Forty-Niner

For the first time in its history, Cal State Long Beach will freeze admissions for undergraduate students on May 1, university officials said.

In the past, applications have been accepted up until August, said Gloria Kapp, interim director of admissions and financial aid.

"We're reducing the number of new students, rather than making those students who are already enrolled have a very difficult time getting the classes they need," Kapp said.

This year, due to budget constraints, all undergraduate applications from transfer students and post-graduate students seeking a second degree will be closed May 1. First-time freshman applications were closed April 15.

The freeze will probably reduce the number of applications for fall '91 by 2,000 to 3,000, and full-time equivalent enrollment by 1,000 to 2,000 students, Kapp said.

The enrollment freeze was decided upon to help relieve classroom congestion, said Frank Alfieri, chairman of the Academic Senate. Budget problems have already resulted in between 500 to 900 class sections being removed from the schedule.

In addition, the Admissi Records Office has impose unit limit on VRR registra continuing students will better chance to get an a number of classes.

"When we know what the will be we can open u classes, and if need be we c up admissions again," Alfi "We're trying to give pri existing students first."

Please see FREEZE—

CALIFORNIA STATE UNIVERSITY, LONG BEACH

OFFICE OF THE PRESIDENT
(213) 985-4121

March 13, 1991

TO: All University Employees

FROM: Curtis L. McCray
President

SUBJECT: Layoff Notification Procedures

Within the last few weeks there has been an increasing amount of rumor, conjecture, discussion and perhaps justifiable concern over the possibility that the current budget crisis may lead to layoff of personnel on campus. It is best to keep this in perspective and not allow these rumors to concern us to the detriment of morale and work performance.

The business of the University will go on as usual while plans are made for dealing with the budget situation. While we will always do our best to find other ways to resolve our problems, no one can promise that there will not be any layoffs at all. However, you are reminded that layoff can occur only when the President announces that such action is necessary, and following extensive consultation with many constituents including bargaining agents for represented employees.

To help us avoid unnecessary worry and control rumors, you are reminded that only the President can make such announcements, and that authority to act as my agent in making announcements of layoffs has not been delegated at this time to any other individual on campus. Therefore, if any other person advises you that you might be or will be laid off, treat that as an unauthorized statement or rumor, and get on with business.

CLM:jo

1250 Bellflower Boulevard Long Beach, California 90840

1990s

THE NINETIES STARTED WITH THE COLLECTIVE BUMMER OF STEEP BUDGET CUTS, the elimination of the football team in 1991, and a battle over sacred land on campus. Things perked up later with the addition of a new, optimistic president in Robert Maxson, the new Walter Pyramid and Carpenter Performing Arts Center, an improving economy, and several sports national championships. The chant "Go Beach!" also became a thing on campus.

PUVUNGNA

The ancient, sacred land known as Puvungna, which occupies twenty-two acres on the west end of campus, has infused the campus identity. Puvungna has at times been a flash point of controversy, as campus officials over the years sought to turn it into a retail space, leave construction debris on it or, most recently, let it be. A 2021 legal settlement brought permanent protection to Puvungna, as well as a guarantee of tribal input on its future stewardship. Puvungna is what remains of a site considered sacred to the Tongva people. It was home to the god Chinigchinich, who was venerated by tribes across the southwest US.

There is ample physical evidence of Native Americans who settled, ate, and lived on the university land roughly 1,000 years ago. According to a May 2013 article in *Pacific Coast Archaeological Society Quarterly*, construction of a parking garage near the Walter Pyramid turned up pottery pieces, stone and bone tools, and more than a metric ton of mollusk shells, a popular dining choice of early Native Americans. The site, dated to 1200 AD to 1700 AD, contained the best-dated excavated pottery collection from Southern California and "reveals a ceramic industry pre-dating the arrival of Europeans," the article states. A 2023 audit of the state's universities found that Long Beach State was the only CSU to repatriate a majority—70 percent—of the ancestral remains found in its collection.

The land, its history, and the struggle to preserve it, has made a huge impact. The campus has been the site of the Pow Wow gathering, which draws thousands of Native Americans to upper campus every spring. The campus also boasts the oldest and one of the largest American Indian Studies departments in the Cal State system.

"Puvungna is the emergence point of the spiritual philosophy of most Southern California Indian tribes. That's the best way to put it. It's where the world emerges and where those creation narratives occur."

—CINDI ALVITRE, American Indian Studies lecturer who oversees NAGPRA (Native American Graves Protection and Repatriation Act, 1990) compliance and repatriation to affiliated tribes

"It's sacred to the Tongva Gabrielino people as well as other California Indians. The influence of the spiritual philosophy extends to northern Baja and out to Arizona. That's why our politics are so complex. There's so many tribal groups. Some federally recognized and some state. It's a super unique site in California. That's the full extent of Chinigchinich religion and philosophy. This is where they emerge from pre-human to human form . . . They become human at Cal State Long Beach."

—CRAIG STONE, professor emeritus of American Indian Studies at Cal State Long Beach

"It is rare in Southern California that the name of a native village has survived into the historic period and that it can be identified with one of the many known archaeological sites. The Gabrielino village of Puvungna is in all probability one of these rare sites."

—KEITH A. DIXON, *Reviving Puvungna—An Archaeological Project at Rancho Los Alamitos*

A ceremony at Puvungna in 2020 and in the 1990s when plans for a retail/housing development on the site drew widespread protests.

The Would-Be Strip Mall

In the 1990s, Native Americans won a bitter court battle against the university to protect Puvungna land. President Curtis McCray, under pressure to raise revenue on campus, had his heart set on a retail and residential plan that would have put shopping right on the site considered sacred by the Tongva people.

Native Americans rallied, aided by neighbors in Park Estates who were afraid of the extra traffic and noise the proposed West Village Center would invariably bring.

"Would the Christian communities allow you to urinate on the Shroud of Turin, or build a mini mall in sacred sites in Jerusalem?" Cindi Alvitre, a Gabrielino-Tongva Indian who later became an activist and lecturer in American Indian Studies at Long Beach State, wrote to interim President Karl Anatol in May 1993. "Well, I say to you . . . our people will not allow this desecration of our sacred sites, either."

As for the development, the university gave up on it soon after President Robert Maxson took office in 1994. Maxson promised the Native American community he would not build on the land while he was president. He didn't say it would never happen, but he said *he* wouldn't do it. And Maxson said later he hated the idea of a strip mall on campus anyway.

DANIELLE SCOTT

Danielle Scott was a six-foot-two volleyball and basketball star from Baton Rouge, Louisiana, who had decided to go to Georgia, when Long Beach State women's volleyball coach Brian Gimmillaro intervened. Scott would lead Long Beach State to its second women's volleyball national championship, in 1993. She was also a rare three-sport athlete, playing basketball for LBSU and running the anchor in the 4x100 relay as well as playing volleyball. After college, the now five-time Olympian moved on to coaching volleyball and in 2023 was recruiting talent for a pro women's volleyball league.

Scott's parents leaned toward Georgia, and Scott and her family had reservations about the LA area.

Danielle Scott (far left) and teammates after beating Penn State to win it all in 1993.

Valley Banks
WHEN PERFORMANCE REALLY COUNTS
NCAA BOXING CHAMPIONS
Beach
9

"

"Georgia was closer . . . All we knew in LA was LA and gangs . . . It was dangerous in LA—the gangs! [Gimmillaro] flew to Louisiana twice: 'No no no no, you have to come to Long Beach.' He was afraid to fly. He made a passionate speech: 'I would have family and him and my team . . . '

It was a complete culture shock and I relied on him and my teammates. I was from a small town. I was very conservative and here I am in California. Everything was different, from the style of clothes to the weather that was beautiful, being near the beach. In Louisiana we have greenery and swamps and big mosquitoes. You have that student athlete built-in support system. And then eventually I found my church family, which has always grounded me.

We didn't have the Pyramid. It was supposed to be done my senior year, but it wasn't. I remember the Gold Mine being cozy. I don't think they had AC—all those fans in there. It was a little hot box . . ."

"We had Long Beach pride with how we walked into the gym and how we presented ourselves. We couldn't have a different colored scrunchy in our hair. I had to line up the creases of my socks. Brian said If you feel good about your look, you'll feel good about your play. Of course, then you'll have to go out and compete. I sooo bought into it. I painted my nails before the games. I smudged my nail once before the game and it was like, 'Oh my God!! I can't believe I did this!' Someone got me some polish right before the game.

We were always about the look. We also wanted to look tough. Even though they weren't injured, we'd get our fingers taped; it was like going into battle. The 1993 national championship match was in Madison, Wisconsin. We battled for that win; we ended up winning in four. Everyone had to step up. While I had a decent match, it was not my best. Last play was me with a block. We did that doggy pile, and everyone fell on top of you.

It took a lot of convincing by Brian that I was going to be taken care of and I was going to have a great career there and all that happened."

—DANIELLE SCOTT

BRIAN GIMMILLARO

"WE HAD A LOT TO DO WITH THAT!"

Brian Gimmillaro coached the Long Beach State women's volleyball team to three national championships in 1989, 1993, and 1998. Future Olympian Misty May (later May-Treanor) led the last championship team with a 36–0 record. May, the daughter of two beach volleyball players, was a top recruit from Newport Harbor High School who one day called Gimmillaro to tell him she wanted to come to Long Beach State.

Tara Cross-Battle led the 1989 team, and Danielle Scott the 1993 team.

Coach Brian Gimmillaro and Misty May before the 1998 championship match.

"[Misty May] was the number one recruit, I was happy to hear it. She was an outside hitter and we made her a setter. She's the best I've seen, and it's been twenty-six years. I've never seen athletes who can do what she did with the ball."

"1989 was maybe most significant because no other team in NCAA history in women's volleyball had won an NCAA championship with more than one woman of color on the team. We won in 1989 with five Black women starters. That was unheard of. It says something about a lot of things. There was an NAACP proclamation about that team. That was a major step in breaking the color barrier. Things changed after that. What did we have to do with that? We had a lot to do with that! There were more women of color playing the game after that."

The 1989 NCAA national championship team.

MISTY MAY AND THE 1998 CHAMPIONSHIP TEAM

Misty May signed on at Long Beach in 1994 for a lot of reasons students do—her parents lived a half hour away in Costa Mesa, and she could eat home-cooked meals and get her laundry done. And her volleyball-player parents could catch her matches. She also fondly remembered the Long Beach summer camps featuring head coach Gimmillaro and Debbie Green, considered one of the nation's top setter's coaches.

"She was by far the best player," Melissa Ohta, a defensive specialist on the team, said of May. "She and Debbie were working every day on something. She kept getting better and better and you didn't think she could get much better."

As setter, May would lecture, cajole, or amuse her teammates so effectively that she became "better than anyone else at making her fellow players better," according to Gimmillaro.

Women's volleyball had already become a force on the Long Beach campus, having won NCAA national championships in 1989 and 1993 behind Tara Cross-Battle and Danielle Scott. But May and the 1998 team gave Long Beach State something it hadn't seen before and hasn't since—a perfect, 36–0 season and an NCAA national championship. Their achievements were rooted in a crushing loss to Stanford in the national semifinal that ended their previous season; the team subsequently grew a volleyball-sized chip on its shoulder. In 1998, tough practices became more brutal, and the team romped through the season, filling the new-ish Walter Pyramid with patrons who got free bagels or In-N-Out burgers if

Beach

The 1998 NCAA champions celebrate after a win over Penn State and a 36-0 record for the season.

the team won in less than sixty minutes. Young girls and middle-aged men showed up at the games in May's signature pigtails.

The 49ers defeated the University of Florida in the NCAA semifinal match to go 35–0. Next up was 35–0 Penn State. The 49ers won the first two games easily, but the Lions came back to win the next two and took an 8–4 lead in the final game. Instead of falling apart, as the team did against Stanford the previous year, the 49ers clawed back.

"We were better prepared and we executed," Gimmillaro said. "We were not gonna come that far and not win. There was no doubt in my mind we were going to win. I had no fear of not winning, no instant of negative thought."

May agreed the team had reached that sweet spot of preparation and battle-tested confidence. "We were like the little train that kept plugging away," she said. "It would have been nice to win in three. We had our chances. We never doubted and we just kept going. There was no panic, there was a calm like everything was going to be fine."

Melissa Ohta, who went on to coach at the University of Arizona, described the feeling as relief. "Everything you did was completely worth it and after being so disappointed the year before, made it twice as good. It was the best feeling . . . that it was all worth it. You don't get to say that often in life."

The 49ers won 15–3, 15–10, 13–15, 14–16, 15–12 in front of 13,194 fans, an NCAA volleyball crowd record that stood for five years. May was named co-MVP of the tournament, setting an NCAA record with twenty service aces. She was also named the American Volleyball Coaches Association (AVCA) player of the year for the second year in a row, the first consecutive AVCA winner since Long Beach State's Tara Cross in 1989–1990.

The team threw out the first pitch at a Dodger's game, and they met President Bill Clinton by Air Force One on the LAX tarmac. May became a superstar in beach volleyball, winning three Olympic gold medals. While she went on to international recognition, May said her 1998 LBSU teammates were special.

"There was nothing like the women I shared college experiences with. As a team we set a goal and everyone made that decision to follow through. Every time I see it, I get goose bumps . . . it meant the world to us and still does."

ROBERT MAXSON

"GO BEACH!"

The CSULB campus Robert Maxson found when he arrived in 1994 could have been described as clinically depressed. The football team had folded in 1991, enrollment was down, and professors were dropping out with golden parachute contracts. Fees were up, and the college and community were reeling from a bad economy and the drawn-out closure of the US Naval shipyard in the mid-1990s.

"When I came it was sort of a tough time and morale was not as high as it should have been. I thought structurally the university was in such good shape but maybe lacked self-confidence." Maxson added: "It just needed a big hug and to be told 'you're good.'"

After decades of skyrocketing enrollments, the number of students fell more than 12 percent from 1992 to 1994, to 26,277—largely because of admission restrictions due to budget cuts. The six-year graduation rate was around 30 percent and courses, sports, and teaching positions were slashed while fees were rising.

Meanwhile, at UNLV, President Maxson had just driven basketball coach Jerry Tarkanian from the program, angering boosters. Maxson was looking for a fresh start when CSULB came calling.

The campus was quickly charmed by the 59-year-old's smooth Arkansas accent, his hugs, and his boundless optimism.

"He came to campus and walked around and said, 'these people are just depressed,'" recalled Doug Robinson, then the vice president of student services.

Maxson set out to promote the campus.

First, he found a rallying cry. He took the "Beach" nickname and ran with it. He started punctuating his speeches with "Go Beach!" He greeted students on campus that way. And they eventually started answering "Go Beach" back.

"I think I recognized it would bring a little pride . . . I'm not sure it made academic departments better," Maxson said, "but I think student morale benefited."

Suddenly, the words "The Beach" started showing up on many a free space on campus—even the water tower at the Veterans Administration hospital next door. Eventually, student body president Robert Garcia asked if the student government could paint "Go Beach" on the bottom of the student union pool. Maxson said fine—if they could find the money. Garcia, who would eventually become mayor of Long Beach and a US Congressional representative, saw to it that the pool was drained, painted, and filled up again.

"They would go to trustees' meetings and our student body president would give a report—'Thank you for having me, and Go Beach!'" Maxson said. "We got known for that 'round the CSU system."

Meanwhile, university number crunchers learned they had been incorrectly submitting graduation and other statistics indicating university health and well-being. They learned to submit numbers that highlighted the university's selling points.

Maxson launched the President's Scholars program in 1994, offering free tuition and housing for select students with high GPAs. The program that he started at UNLV, after getting a casino magnate to donate, was bringing more top students to the LBSU campus. More scholars landed on campus, and university officials learned that students who didn't get in on a full scholarship would enroll anyway and "ride the coattails of the President's Scholars," Robinson said.

"He walked the walk, and talked the talk," said Valerie Bordeaux, who ran the President's Scholars program for years. "He made it a priority, every meeting he led and every organization he spoke to, he was talking about that program."

Chris Lowe, director of the Shark Lab on campus, said Maxson was constantly seen around campus. "He'd . . . just sit down with a bunch of students and just start talking to them. Plus, you know, he was a consummate fundraiser. People don't talk about that as much."

Slowly, the median campus age came down, and more students started seeing The Beach as a destination, rather than a school of convenience.

Maxson said that when he arrived at Long Beach State it was "mainly known as a university of part-time students, a university of older students. Both of those are fine; we cherish those returning students. We just wanted our share of the best and brightest. If you're always the third or fourth choice, you're never going to be a very good university."

University enrollment beefed up again in the late nineties, and the school started to appear in the *U.S. News & World Report* rankings.

Relations between faculty and the president's office, which had been rocky and occasionally hostile for decades, smoothed considerably during the Maxson years. When he retired, the president of the academic senate made a joke about cloning him.

Maxson "doesn't get near enough credit for changing the culture of the campus," said Scott Charmack, who spent twenty-five years with facilities and physical planning.

"We were a sleeping giant, and he woke us up," says Bordeaux. "He gave those hugs and told the stories, and he woke us up."

THE PRESIDENT'S SCHOLARS PROGRAM

In 1995, when Robert Maxson announced the President's Scholars program that would offer high school valedictorians a chance to attend Long Beach State for free, faculty members were skeptical. "We were thinking, 'How's he going to get valedictorians to come to CSULB?'" recalls Dee Abrahamse, then the associate dean of the College of Liberal Arts. "They're going to go to UCLA and Berkeley."

Students weren't much more receptive, but enough of them came around. Maxson introduced the first President's Scholars class (of 1994) of ten students in the Student Union ballrooms in the fall of 1995. "They got a standing ovation," recalls Valerie Bordeaux, who ran the program.

The first President's Scholars class of 1994.

"Everyone went wild." Maxson made sure to include parents in the ceremony.

"He understood the sports concept where you recruit the family, not just the students," vice president of student services Doug Robinson said. "He'd have all those parents up there and drip honey on them just as he dripped honey on the students. He was playing to the university community . . ."

The program was folded into the University Honors program in 2015 and became the President's Scholarship. By the 2020s it was still considered a top scholarship program for the university, offering approximately twenty incoming students free tuition and housing, according to President Jane Close Conoley.

> "[Long Beach State] was not my first option. I wanted UCI. Everybody likes the UCs. Cal State Long Beach—I wasn't even considering it. It was closer to home, but it wasn't like, "Oh my gosh, that's my number one choice." Once you meet President Maxson, you're on board with everything he says. He's an inspiration. He said, "We're gonna bring in the best and the brightest." I was one of the best and brightest! These people around me [in the program] are geniuses. I'm in company with them, and I'm from Jordan High!
>
> —**DIANNE ASIS,** a member of the first President's Scholars class

ROBERT GARCIA

Robert Garcia arrived at Long Beach State in 1995 from the San Gabriel Valley. He had been down to Mother's Beach in Long Beach with his parents and thought the campus "enormous." He initially wanted to be a journalist and cover government and politicians, but then decided he wanted to be a part of the government and become a political leader.

He joined Associated Students, Inc. and became student body president in 1999. According to an article in the *Daily Forty-Niner*, Garcia promoted the "Pyramid plan." He wanted to get concerts for students and make the Pyramid a venue rivaling San Diego State's Cox Arena. "We got Smash Mouth the first year. We got a bunch of other concerts. We worked on it."

But even more important for Garcia was that he forged a strong relationship with President Robert Maxson. He called the president the best mentor he ever had.

"I never forget what he once said. He said you can will yourself to be happy. That really stuck with me. It's one thing he taught me which I used my whole life . . . You can really do that."

Garcia picked up Maxson's sunny "Go Beach!" mantra and ran with it. He successfully lobbied to paint "Go Beach!" on the floor of the USU pool, among other places. He made a "Go Beach!" flag, which the college framed and gave to him. "I certainly got that the brand was developing. When I was mayor that became my thing. We had the *Go Beach!* newsletter. I transferred that from CSULB."

Garcia, who served two terms as Long Beach mayor, was elected to Congress in 2022 and, despite the many dramas of Capitol Hill, maintains himself as a "positive person." He says he understands "Congress is a place you have to be aggressive. We cannot allow a steamrolling back of gay rights or women's rights. You have to be in a position to push back. I wish it wasn't the case, but it is."

He called Long Beach State "one of the best things that ever happened to me. It was my first Long Beach address. It's where I gave my first speech and last speech as mayor."

THE WALTER PYRAMID

- Opened: November 30, 1994, when the men's basketball team hosted Detroit
- Cost: $22 million
- Chief benefactor: Mike and Arlene Walter, who kicked in $2 million, prompting others to contribute. Walter was vice president of Levi Strauss & Co., a popular professor, and dean of the College of Business Administration from 1993–2000.
- Architect: Donald Gibbs, who designed the Carpenter Center and the psychology buildings on campus. Donald's father, Hugh, drew up Long Beach State's first campus master plan in the mid-1950s.
- Backstory: The 1978 master plan called for some kind of arena on the northern end of campus. The state had only recently—in 1988—started allowing money to flow to "PE projects" as opposed to strictly academic ones. Several PE projects were approved on campus in 1990. However, voters refused to pass a bond to finance them. That meant the buildings would have to be done cheaply or not at all.
- Campus officials, aware that the athletic department was tired of the sweaty and cramped Gold Mine Gym, were willing to try. School officials visited arenas in Berkeley, Davis, Irvine,

and San Jose. The Long Beach State athletic director at the time suggested moving the geodesic dome used to house the Spruce Goose aircraft. They considered a domed arena. All ideas ended up being far too costly. Donald Gibbs drew up plans for an arena that would seat 7,500 (but only about 5,000 seats went in, to save money). The seats would be close to the court and, at the request of Jon Regnier, the campus head of facilities, hydraulic lifts would be installed for the seats, eliminating time spent pulling out bleachers as was the procedure for every Gold Mine contest.

- Fun facts: Homeowners who initially complained about the Pyramid have since learned to live with, and even like, the sky-blue monolith in their midst. "If you talk to people who were freaked out about it being across the street from their homes, they'd say now they kind of like it," said Andy Jones, a neighbor who helped fight the building and later moved to associate vice chancellor and deputy general counsel for the Cal State system. "It's kind of a landmark, 'Hey I live by the Pyramid.'" The Pyramid can be seen from every point on campus and the local freeways, and quickly became a symbol of the university. It appeared on letters, Christmas cards, and on the masthead of the campus newspaper. It became a symbol of the neighborhood; a local realtor put it on his truck.
- Downside: A contractor over-drilled fasteners to the roof and another contractor installed the corrugated steel with seams on the bottom, allowing water to leak in. This prompted rounds of litigation and necessitated thousands of dollars in repairs. The blue roof was designed to last twenty-five years. In 2023, the university commissioned a study on the feasibility of repairing the roof, which was seeing increasing leaks—enough to push games into the old Gold Mine Gym in winter 2023.
- The Walter Pyramid has definitely started showing its age, with frequent leaks: "Tens of thousands of potential leak points," Mark Zakhour, vice president of Beach Building Services, told the *Daily Forty-Niner*. The venue hosted the 2024 NCAA men's volleyball tournament, but its long-term future was up in the air.

In 2006, an increasingly diverse student population protested the country's border policies as well as sharply rising tuition hikes.

2000s

THE NEW CENTURY BROUGHT PROTESTS, TUITION INCREASES, trauma from the September 11 attacks but also more building, more research recognition, and more national championships in men's volleyball. The pandemic would shutter the campus in 2020 and 2021.

Daily 49er

Since 1949

2 Business as usual in the residence halls on campus.

3 Wayne Stickney-Smith calls for a campus-wide town hall meeting in the aftermath of Tuesday's attacks.

5 Student speak out in the wake of terrorist acts.

VOL. LII, NO. 11 CALIFORNIA STATE UNIVERSITY, LONG BEACH WEDNESDAY, SEPTEMBER 12, 2001

The Unthinkable

Tom Horan/AP

The Pentagon burns after a plane crashed through an outer wall during a terrorist attack Tuesday morning.

A Message from the President to the Campus Community

Subject: **A Message from the President to the Campus Community**
Date: Wed, 12 Sep 2001 11:45:02 -0700 (PDT)
From: "President Robert Maxson" <president@csulb.edu>
To: CSULB Faculty and Staff - List Supressed <nobody@csulb.edu>

In the wake of yesterday's events, I know all of us share a deep sympathy for all of those families who have been touched by this tragedy.

Cal State Long Beach is a university that has always stood as an outstanding model of the American ideal. We have always reached out to every person without regard to religion or cultural heritage. Our campus is a community where a highly diverse population lives, learns and works in an atmosphere of tolerance, civility and respect.

I ask that all of us recognize the rights and the feelings of every American member and every international member of our campus community, and that we ensure that no one feels any discomfort here in the difficult days ahead.

Because these are extraordinary times, I have asked our professional and psychological staff offices to be open and available for anyone who may need assistance.

On a personal note, I want to thank all of you for the manner in which you handled the situation during yesterday.s first tragic hours. I look forward to seeing you on campus.

Warmest Personal Regards,
Bob Maxson

Subject: **Counseling Services Available**
Date: Thu, 13 Sep 2001 07:22:00 -0700
From: "Sara Sluss" <sbsluss@csulb.edu>
To: lib-all-personnel@csulb.edu

Colleagues,
FYI.
Sara
==
----- Forwarded by Sara Sluss/AcademicAffairs/CSULB on 09/13/01 07:24 AM -----

"Maryan St. Claire" <stclaire@csulb.edu>
09/12/01 08:53 AM

To: Chairs-all@csulb.edu
cc: "Pamela E. Ashe" <peashe@csulb.edu>
Subject: Counseling Services Available

To: Department Chairs
Student Services Directors

From: Clyde Crego, Director
Counseling and Psychological Services

Please have faculty and staff announce the following message to all students:

Professionals from Counseling and Psychological Services, Department of Social Work,
University Interfaith Center and Career Development Center will be available for students
who need to talk about the current traumatic events in two locations:

University Student Union Room 225
Sept. 13, 2001, Thursday
9:00 a.m. ? 5:00 p.m.

Counseling and Psychological Services
Brotman Hall Room 226
8:00 a.m. ? 5:00 p.m.
Everyday (Monday-Friday)

Thank you.

1 of 2 9/13/01 9:04 AM

The September 11, 2001, attacks shut down the campus for a day.

Austin Lewis

Austin Lewis was an undeclared freshman living at Residence Commons, Building D, on September 11, 2001.

"

My alarm clock went off and it was playing a news broadcast instead of the radio morning show that should have been on the air. I thought that was odd, but I shrugged and turned it off without paying attention to what they were saying. I showered and got ready for my day, and I found out about the attack when I checked the news on my computer before going to the dining hall for breakfast. My morning class was English 100, and we spent the whole period talking about what was going on. Some of my classmates were in the student union earlier that morning and saw the second plane crash live on TV. I first heard about Flight 93 crashing in Pennsylvania from another classmate. I remember Osama bin Laden's name coming up a lot, even that early in the day.

Campus officially closed a few hours later. Everyone I talked to was feeling uneasy because campus police found a suspicious vehicle or a suspicious package in one of the parking lots. And we were all wondering if there was going to be another attack at the World Trade Center in downtown Long Beach. Back at my dorm that afternoon, we were all watching the news on our TVs. A group of about ten of us were getting together to go donate blood, but then we heard on the news that there were long lines at hospitals and they were telling people to stay home. Long Beach Airport's flight path goes over CSULB, so one other detail I remember is how quiet the campus was on 9/11 and over the next couple days because the FAA had grounded all flights. But in the dorms, we'd still hear a plane every now and then, and we'd freeze in the middle of whatever we were doing until we could convince ourselves it was safe.

Bonnie Gasior

Bonnie Gasior was a newly hired professor of Spanish in 2001, and had been living in California for a month.

"

I was still finding my bearings personally and professionally as a freshly minted PhD with only a few acquaintances and no family in the area. I recall waking up that morning in my one-bedroom apartment in Belmont Shore and hard-swallowing the first stunning images on the news. It felt unreal, impossible, horrifying. I literally pinched myself. Although instinctually I wanted to stay glued to the TV for developing information, I had a Tuesday/Thursday teaching schedule that term. I drove to campus in a haze. I was met by a police officer in the parking lot, who told me campus was closed and classes cancelled as a precautionary measure. It became clear at that moment we were at war, and that this gaping wound would leave a deep scar on the country.

I returned home, hoping to be able to gain some understanding of the incomprehensible. I found myself feeling helpless and hopeless, as I watched the planes hit the towers repeatedly. It took my breath away in the worst way possible . . .

I didn't leave my apartment for most of that day. I remember thinking "I should walk to a coffee shop" only to be met with feelings of unworthiness and guilt. How could I even consider enjoying a coffee when others lost loved ones today? I thought and still think, especially on anniversaries, about all the people who said goodbye to their children and spouses that morning, never realizing it would be their last time.

STEVEN SPIELBERG

Steven Spielberg was a Long Beach State film student in the mid-1960s. He left after three years, when he got a job in the film industry. The director of *Schindler's List*, *Jaws*, and *E.T.* returned in 2001 to finish the bachelor's degree work he started. Registering under an assumed name, and known to only a handful of faculty, he submitted the Oscar-winning *Schindler's List* to pass the advanced filmmaking class. Spielberg also filed a paper to complete his general education requirement, according to a 2002 article in the *Los Angeles Times*. Spielberg walked with a body-guard and thousands of other undergrads at the May 31, 2002, graduation ceremony. He shook hands and high-fived fellow grads on his way to the stage. When his name was called, the band struck up the theme music from *Raiders of the Lost Ark*. President Robert Maxson told the media then that Spielberg wanted his children to know he got his degree—in his case, thirty-three years later.

Steven Spielberg was the center of attention at the 2002 CSULB graduation.

F. KING ALEXANDER

"GRADUATION BEGINS TODAY"

When he came to campus in 2006 to succeed retiring President Robert C. Maxson, F. King Alexander saw a healthy campus that he felt needed some more financial love from the state of California. "At most major universities, recruitment is an issue, but not here. Revenue was an issue," he said years later.

"Ninety-nine percent of our students were in-state students. I told them if you continue to cut our budget, I'm going to get every kid in Nebraska to come here [and pay out-of-state tuition] because we have 'beach' in our name. We're the only major public university with 'beach' in our name. You can scour the country and you won't find one."

While his predecessor, Robert Maxson, liked to stay closer to campus, Alexander flew to Washington, D.C., monthly to represent the Cal States with policies and Pell Grants. "I was always a policy guy." The goal was to get graduation numbers up.

"We broke record after record. On napkins in the dining halls we had 'Graduation Begins Today.' It's not about going to college anymore; it's about finishing college. The worst thing you can do to a student is let them drop out . . . They have debt, no degree and have probably given up on a part-time job and had earnings losses." The six-year graduation rate was 42 percent in 2006 and rose to about 70 percent by the 2020s.

The Kentucky-raised Alexander was known as a basketball fan who often played ball with students on campus. A fan of the Midnight Basketball program, the president played pickup games

Incoming CSULB president F. King Alexander greets outgoing president Robert Maxson in 2006. Maxson retired after almost twelve years at the helm.

at Long Beach Poly High School. "Once, the Poly coach leaned over and said, 'your two man is a Crip and three man is a Blood.' I'm like, okay, I'll start passing the ball more."

The $110 million Hall of Science and the $70 million Student Recreation and Wellness Center went up on Alexander's watch. He also lobbied the Obama administration to allow federal stimulus money to flow to education when the 2008 financial crisis brought the Hall of Science project to a halt. "We had a hole in the ground, and we were thirty days from laying off three hundred construction workers on that site," he said. He also worked with Long Beach City College and Long Beach Unified to sign the Long Beach College Promise, allowing qualifying local students a path to competitive Long Beach State. Then-governor Jerry Brown eventually signed the College Promise into law in 2017.

"We didn't blame anybody for test scores that didn't match up. Every kid in Long Beach was our kid." Alexander is particularly proud Long Beach State continues to score high on social mobility rankings, including number one in 2023 in *U.S. News & World Report.*

In 2013, Alexander went to Louisiana State University as chancellor and president, then on to Oregon State, where controversy followed him, leading to his resignation in 2021. In 2023, he was in Washington, D.C., lobbying for the College Promise Foundation and the Department of Education on the "Free Community College" movement. He became a professor at Florida Gulf Coast University, teaching graduate students higher education finance, policy, and law.

He said Long Beach State was his favorite of the four public schools he has led. Was it a mistake to leave Long Beach for LSU?

"My wife will tell you that. That was a tough decision. [CSU Chancellor] Charlie Reed thought if I wanted to stay with the Cal States, I'd get his position . . . I had twelve years under my belt as a president, five at Murray State, seven-and-a-half at Long Beach State. When she's mad at me, Shenette [Alexander's wife] says, 'You should have stayed in Long Beach.'"

LONG BEACH STATE PRESIDENTS

P. Victor Peterson, July 1949–June 1959

Interim: Henry Magnuson, July–August 1959

Carl McIntosh, September 1959–February 1969

Acting: Donald H. Simonsen, February 1969–July 1970

Stephen Horn, August 1970–February 1988

Acting: June Cooper, February–May 1988

Curtis McCray, May 1988–January 1993

Interim: Karl Anatol, January 1993–May 1994

Robert Maxson, June 1994–January 2006

F. King Alexander, January 2006–June 2013

Interim: Donald Para, July 2013–June 2014

Jane Close Conoley, July 2014–present

JANE CLOSE CONOLEY

When she started in 2014, Jane Close Conoley, the first woman appointed as president (non-interim), found the campus "in really good shape" and tipped her hat to her predecessors, Robert Maxson and F. King Alexander.

Maxson was known as a president who stayed close to campus and seemed to know virtually every person walking it. F. King Alexander was a policy expert who would fly to Washington D.C. and Sacramento regularly to lobby for more funding for higher education. Conoley wanted to try to run somewhere in the middle.

"Alexander was absolutely a kind of a national expert on higher ed funding, so he would have a special focus on that. I was more focused on the interpersonal climate that I was entering . . . I did think I needed to be a combination of Maxson and Alexander. I needed to be working on the national reputation of Cal State Long Beach.

"We weren't quite getting the national recognition that we deserved, and it was because we weren't putting out stories about who we were . . . getting it out there about social mobility, and moving to R2 (high research activity) status, and being called the best bang for the buck. Nobody gets that unless you put yourself out there—and then people start looking at your data."

The Basic Needs program to help low-income students, the Rapid Rehousing program, and various emergency grants for students were established under Conoley to help students in a housing market where costs continue to escalate. The "No Barriers" campaign aims to limit barriers to graduation, including bureaucratic and economic ones. Encouraging the police force to focus on de-escalation became a priority, especially after the murder of George Floyd in 2020.

"Interacting with police is very tricky for many of our students who come from areas where they have been harassed and maybe abused by police . . . There's no one thing that would make a huge difference. But internally, that was certainly my focus." Police Chief John Brockie was hired in 2022 and has worked to prioritize campus outreach.

The Shakarian Family Student Success Center, the Bob Murphy Access Center, the Professional and Continuing Education building, the Anna W. Ngai Alumni Center, and Parkside North—the first new dorm in 34 years—all went up during Conoley's time.

The COVID pandemic was perhaps the biggest crisis of Conoley's administration. CSULB, like a lot of places, planned to stay closed for two weeks in March 2020, but that time limit stretched to 14 months. "There were many surprises along the way."

With serious concerns about students and staff getting sick, students and faculty stayed masked for months. One baseball team party violated the rules in the early days of COVID. "We had to help them get healthy but then also teach them a lesson. It was kind of a marathon of problems to solve. We looked into whether we could test wastewater. But we didn't have the right system to do that. All of our wastewater went into one pipe . . . so we wouldn't be able to tell where we might have clusters of infections. In my worst moments, I thought, *This is really a lot.* And then in my best moments, I thought, *Not many other presidents will get to say they led during a pandemic, so I guess I should just run with it and see what I can learn.*"

PARA
MI
FAMILIA
CSULB
California State University
Long Beach

MAULANA KARENGA

Professor Maulana Karenga led an initiative to fight the planned diminution of the Africana Studies department to a smaller program in 2013. That fight led to student demonstrations, community and, eventually, positive legislative action. The Africana Studies professor worked with the CSU Council on Ethnic Studies to get Ethnic Studies made into a general education requirement for all California CSUs.

Karenga, the professor and chair of the Department of Africana Studies, is perhaps best known for creating the African American and Pan-African holiday Kwanzaa in 1966. The Kwanzaa holiday, which is a celebration of family, community, and culture, runs from December 26 to January 1 and is observed around the world. The holiday, he said, stresses "kinship with other human beings, especially the oppressed and struggling peoples of the world, but also just human beings in general."

Karenga said he continues to get emails, postcards, video clips and photos from people all over the world who celebrate Kwanzaa. A professor at Long Beach State since 1989, he also hears from former students.

"Almost all of them say that 'having your class was a life changing event for me. It gave me a grounding. It taught me to see myself, my people, and the world in a whole new light. And it reaffirmed my confidence in myself. And it made me think more about my culture, and what we have achieved and contributed to American and world history.'

"So that's what I try as best I can, to always, always reaffirm the people in the beauty of themselves, the sacredness of themselves, the soulfulness, and resourcefulness of themselves."

The relatively low proportion of Black students on campus in the 2020s, approximately 3 percent, is a concern for Karenga. He said he is encouraged that college administrators are addressing the issue.

"I am anxious, and I'm committed to increasing it. And I believe that Provost Karyn Scissum Gunn is very involved in this in a way that's significant to what we're trying to do and what we eventually have to do. If we're going to claim equity, if we're going to claim diversity, equity, and inclusion, and excellence, we can't do that without Black people present.

". . . I think the priority requirement for students is student presence. And when students are present, they create a synergy. They create a community where they can collaborate and support each other."

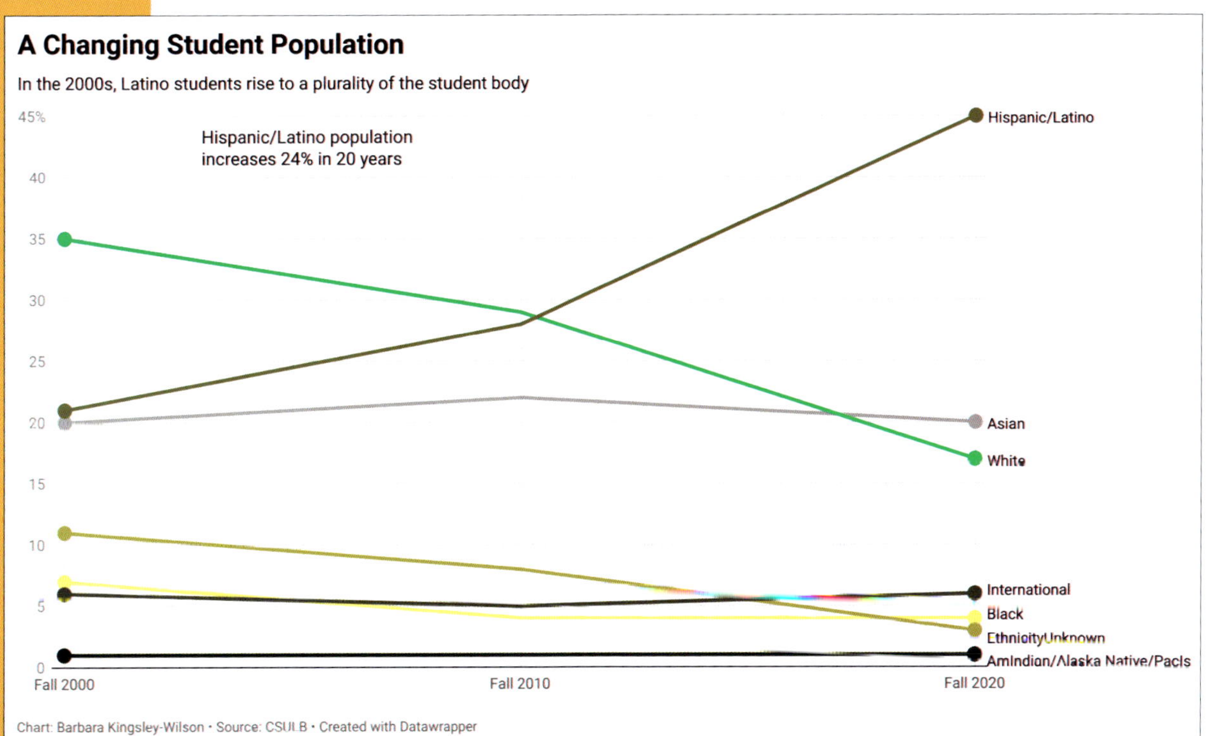

NICKNAMES AND MASCOTS

1950–2018

49ers

Mascot: Prospector Pete

1980s–90s

"The Beach" starts getting popular as a nickname

2020

Elbee the Shark becomes the campus mascot

A growing awareness of the violent history of the Gold Rush "49ers" in relation to Native Americans eventually prompted the university to move away from the 49er moniker and embrace the "Beach" name by 2018. The Shark mascot was added in 2020.

The *Daily Forty-Niner* students also launched plans for a newspaper rebranding. The newspaper will be called the *Long Beach Current*, starting in fall 2024.

Students voted to raise fees to build their own Student Recreation and Wellness Center, which opened to much fanfare, in 2010.

ALAN KNIPE

Alan Knipe had the unique experience of coaching and playing on national championship teams for Long Beach State. He was a second-team all-American volleyball player who helped lead LBSU to an NCAA national championship in 1991. He went on to coach the men's team, taking a break to coach the US men's squad from 2009–2012. He returned to The Beach, and his teams kept getting stronger and better, making it into the Final Four in 2017 before winning the national championship in 2018 and again in 2019. The former was against UCLA at home and the latter was at the Walter Pyramid before a sold-out crowd.

“

“I remember bits and pieces of it [the 2018 championship], it’s kind of a big blur to be honest. After winning a national championship in ’91 with your teammates, it’s one of the most special things but for the bond you’ll have for the rest of your life. My ’91 guys and I are incredibly close. Very rarely does it drift to ’91 and this play or that game. Just this achievement that you’ve done something unique as a group . . . Every team wants to win the last game and we got to do it. I have this deep-down feeling of wanting my players to feel this feeling.

Well, I think like everything in life, the difference (between playing on a national championship team and coaching one) is you don’t know what you don’t know when you’re 21 or 20 years old. And that is, it’s when you go in it’s so emotional. And it’s an explosion of competitiveness and emotions because of all the physical commitment you put into it. And you just got done really competing, go into battle out there and you let it all out. And it’s very, it’s very emotional, and it’s the high of the high.

And I think the difference of a coach is that even though there are some of those same feelings, I think you realize . . . how hard it is to achieve this goal, much more than you understand it as a player . . . And I think you have a much better perspective on how important it is; not just the emotional exhilaration in the moment, but the impact it’s going to have on these young men’s lives, you know, for the rest of their life, for their relationships, their closeness with the university . . . you become very much like a parent at a graduation . . . You’re just so proud.

. . . You don’t realize as a player . . . how much goes into a college national championship. So when you see the look in, you know, President Conoley’s face or, [then athletic director] Andy Fee’s face or our senior staff . . . It’s just so invigorating and uplifting for the whole campus, that you’re just so happy for everybody.

. . . I hope the next coach wins, five or six or seven national championships and I’ll be the guy down there at the sandbar clapping.”

—ALAN KNIPE

NICK AMADO

Nick Amado had played volleyball at Orange Coast College for two years when coach Alan Knipe walked into practice and asked if he wanted to come play for Long Beach State. It made sense for Amado, who "wasn't thinking of anything else." His mother and uncle went to the school, and he ended up living in Long Beach after college.

After a tough start and redshirting twice after his mother's death and a knee injury, he helped lead The Beach to national championships in 2018 and 2019. He went on to play for a year in Spain and to coach at Golden West College.

Nick Amado spiking the ball against
UCLA in the 2018 championship match.

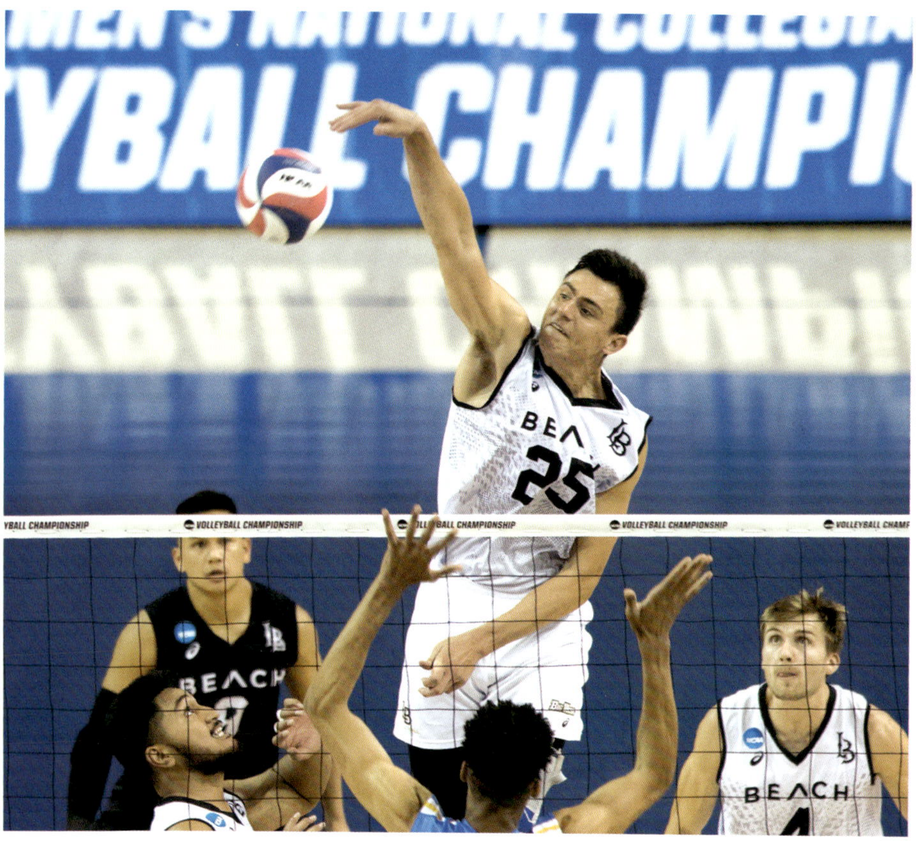

CHAMPS!

Men's volleyball team ends a 20-year drought with a national title. Coverage, pages 6-9.

The *Daily Forty-Niner* newspaper front page showing players celebrating after beating UCLA in Westwood to win the NCAA national championship in 2018.

“

“ . . . Going into [2018], we graduated a lot of guys . . . it was a rebuilding year. We had our seniors coming up. It was TJ [DeFalco], Kyle [Ensing] and Josh [Tuaniga] who got a lot of playing time and a lot of us who were very, very hungry . . .

We were down two-to-one in sets and losing 17–13 in fourth. If you're down four points, at champ level is hard, you gotta make stops on defense, I was matched up with this guy named Gemma . . . He was like this freak athlete. He touched over 12 feet and was almost impossible to deal with.

We touched the ball a couple times and slowed them down. He had twenty kills. As a middle blocker getting twenty kills is absurd. They're only in half the game. The fact that he was getting as many as he did, you gotta clap your hands [and] say, kudos.

. . . We never hung our heads, we just kept fighting. We were a little shocked at first that we got behind. But hey, they're UCLA, like they're kind of good at everything they do.

I got the final kill. I just remembered turning around and screaming. Next thing I know, Ryan Poole is in my arms and the fans stormed the court. I don't think I've ever felt joy in such a pure form like that . . .

We got escorted by the cops [to an East Long Beach sports bar]. My whole family was there, a bunch of alumni were there. I might have cried.”

—NICK AMADO

STUDENT SUCCESS CENTER OPENS

A merging of old campus and new came to fruition when the Shakarian Family Student Success Center opened in January 2019. The $45 million center was created in the footprint of the demolished Peterson Hall 2 science building, built in 1955. The new center brought together key student services—including the Bob Murphy Access Center, the University Center for Undergraduate Advising, and the Educational Opportunity Program—that had been housed in offices all over campus.

The Bob Murphy Access Center, formerly Disabled Student Services, celebrated its fiftieth anniversary in October 2023. Long Beach City Councilmember Mary Zendejas (left) was one of five former students inducted into the center's new Hall of Fame. Zendejas had polio as an infant and uses a wheelchair: "They gave me the confidence to pursue everything I wanted, to keep moving forward," Zendejas, a 2001 graduate, said during the fiftieth anniversary celebration."They taught me that my ability is stronger than my disability."

2022: THE UNIVERSITY ART MUSEUM EXPANDS

The $24 million project included the expansion of the University Art Museum by 4,000 square feet—more than doubling the exhibit space. A multimillion-dollar gift by Carolyn Campagna Kleefeld made the renovation possible. The museum was renamed the Carolyn Campagna Kleefeld Contemporary Art Museum, or the Kleefeld Contemporary for short. The addition created modern spaces for more galleries, work, and educational areas. There's also a field trip program that brings in 1,500 Long Beach area students a year.

An LA art writer criticized the fact that the gift funded a gallery for Kleefeld's work. Paul Baker Prindle, the museum director who oversaw the expansion, said the criticism missed the big picture, and the gift continues to be transformative for the museum.

"The gift agreement has a number of stipulations, like all gift agreements, and one of them was that she wanted to fund the construction of a gallery in the new building where her work could be shown. And she gifted work to the museum. And of course, when you gift your own work it's not tax deductible. . . . What made it a transformative gift and the biggest impact is not having a gallery with her name on it and her work in it. It's that she paid essentially for the entire new building. There's an endowed fund and we have no unpaid interns anymore.

"We also have an operating endowment that we never had before and we just don't really have money problems because of her . . . A lot of people don't realize this, but you know, the Whitney Museum in New York was actually founded in the same way. Gertrude Vanderbilt Whitney was an artist. And you know, she found a museum and it had her stuff in it, and it had to be shown. And now you know, one hundred years later, nobody talks about that."

CAROLYN
CAMPAGNA KLEEFELD
CONTEMPORARY
ART MUSEUM

RASHIDA CRUTCHFIELD

When she was a doctoral student in educational leadership in 2009, Rashida Crutchfield decided to do her dissertation on student homelessness. That wasn't surprising. Crutchfield had worked at a shelter for youth who were unhoused. As a volunteer coordinator at Covenant House in Hollywood, she knew people without stable homes didn't always fit into people's perceived notions. Sometimes they were college students.

Crutchfield's research eventually showed that over 10 percent of Cal State students faced housing insecurity, and as many as one in four struggled to get enough food. She was seeing it at Covenant

House and increasingly in her classrooms as well at Long Beach State. Students were struggling because they were hungry; they were sleeping on friends' couches and weren't sure where they would get their next meal.

Crutchfield noticed among her peers a "bell curve of reaction" to the increased issues of student housing and food insecurity.

"On one end, there were people who were saying things like, 'Yeah, we've been seeing this for a long time. I keep food in my desk, or, as a dean, I tried to sort of counsel students who were trying to figure out how to patch [together] services.' On the other end of the bell were people who were like, 'This is not our job. This is not something we should have to deal with. We're not a social service agency. We're here to educate people.'

"In the middle were a lot of people who understood that there was an issue, who were coming to that realization—but really didn't know what to do about it."

The CSU-wide Basic Needs Program was grounded in Crutchfield's research. The findings from the 2016 and 2018 studies on student basic needs prompted the chancellor's office to hire a staff person to coordinate the Basic Needs Program system-wide. There was an increase in campuses adding food pantries and allowing the use of EBT cards when purchasing food on campus. There's now an emergency housing needs office at Long Beach State to help students with short-term housing.

"People presume that if someone looks a certain way, then they're homeless . . . There's an assumption that if someone is in college, that they likely have all the resources they need to be there. But for many of our students . . . they're working double-hard, triple-hard just to get to college so that they can try to stabilize after college."

Crutchfield, now an associate professor at Long Beach State, extended her research to community-college students in 2023.

"I think it's our job to . . . respond with the urgency of our students, but also to reflect on what's working to make sure that we get it right."

CHRIS LOWE

Chris Lowe was working at a field station in Cape Cod, conducting research, in the 1980s when he learned about this "guy from California . . . doing telemetry on horseshoe crabs." Lowe recognized Don Nelson, the "shark guy" of Cal State Long Beach, founder of the Shark Lab, who made appearances on National Geographic TV and Mutual of Omaha's *Wild Kingdom*.

Nelson, who pioneered the use of acoustic telemetry to study sharks, convinced Lowe, then 23, to come west to Long Beach State to pursue his master's in biology. He met his future wife, Gwen Goodmanlowe, a marine biologist, at Long Beach. Lowe had $200 to his name. "I was adventurous back in those days," Lowe said.

He and Gwen got their PhDs at the University of Hawaii and got married. Then Nelson, who launched the program at Long Beach State in 1966, died in 1997. Lowe was hired to teach marine biology and run the Shark Lab.

"I have no idea how, but I got hired as his replacement. I mean, I hadn't even finished my PhD yet. You really don't get hired in my field unless you have postdoctoral experience. It was a risk hiring someone like me."

Lowe has continued to build the Shark Lab, now one of the largest shark research programs in the world. He's attracted $11 million in funding over the years and been quoted in too many media outlets to count.

Lowe found his niche at CSULB by carving "a path that just hadn't been carved here before." He says the notoriety of the lab helps him get more grant money and other resources that are hard to come by at a "teaching-first CSU like Long Beach State."

Chris Lowe in 1990 hoisting an underwater acoustic speaker for playing back sounds to see what frequencies sharks can hear.

In 2018, he worked with then-assemblymember Patrick O'Donnell to secure $3.75 million for the shark program over five years. O'Donnell helped tuck the money in the CSU allocation, assuring that Long Beach State would get the money and not share it with other programs, like Stanford, that were keen to get it.

"I get a call saying 'Congratulations, you're getting $3.75 million.' So next thing I know we're having meetings with the administration saying, how are we going to do this? We've never done this before, right? It's a lot of money."

The money helped the lab buy drones and other equipment. In 2023, the lab released a study documenting that sharks are much more prevalent and much closer to swimmers and surfers than we imagined.

"We've . . . been telling people this for two decades, that chances are there are sharks around," Lowe said. "You just don't know it. Problem is nobody's ever been able to actually quantify that. It's never been quantified. Now we have for the very first time."

The lab recruits other departments on campus to study the economic impacts of shark scares on local tourism and human behavior around and in reaction to sharks, which also includes creating student art of sharks.

Lowe said he didn't get involved in the choice of Elbee, the shark mascot, chosen by students in 2019 to replace Prospector Pete as the campus mascot.

"I stayed out of it," he said. "My students were all excited about it . . . You know, there are no Division I Sharks in the country. It would be unique, right? And we're The Beach. So that was it. That was my only input. I didn't lobby for it because I'm an alum from the 49er days, right? And every time I give a talk where there's an alumnus, I always get asked 'Are you happy with the mascot?' And I say, 'Well, it's hard for me not to be.'"

Don Nelson, the first LBSU shark expert, at his office in the 1970s. Nelson was one of the first shark biologists and his work was funded by the Office of Naval Research, which was looking for shark repellants for the military, said Chris Lowe. Nelson was known as the world's expert on shark behavior.

Have a Happy

COVID COMES TO CAMPUS

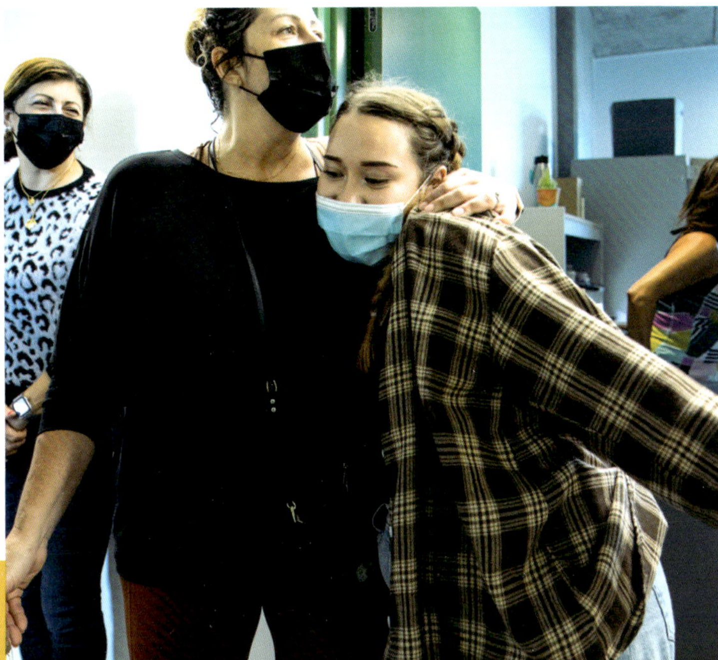

WEEKLY PRINT EDITION

DAILY FORTY-NINER

EST ▲ 1949

Vol. LXXI, Issue 25 www.daily49er.com Sunday, March 15, 2020

CANCELED

Face-to-face classes at CSULB move to 'alternative instruction' due to threats of coronavirus.

Long Beach State officials announced that face-to-face instruction will be canceled from March 12 through March 17 and "alternative instruction" will begin March 18 and will conclude April 20.

"We'll probably give a pause to face-to-face classes for a few days to give professors a chance to figure out how you will deliver your classes remotely and then from a period of two to four weeks after that we will be delivering remotely," Presiden Jane Close Conoley told the Forty-Niner in a March 9 interview.

The decision comes as four coronavirus cases have been confirmed in Long Beach. CSULB's temporary closure marks what other California State University University of California campuses are doing in response to the growing threat of COVID-19.

"This action is a proactive step being taken because of our commitment to your health and safety and supports the concept of 'social distancing,'" Conoley wrote in an campus-wide email. "As the number of cases grow in Los Angeles County, this step very well may save lives and it is on the advice of our medical professionals that we take this step."

Although face-to-face instruction will be moved to online, Conoley said the campus will not be closing.

"Campus offices and buildings will remain open and many operations will continue normally, including student housing and related dining facilities," she said. "Students who need computers or WiFi will find appropriate resources on campus in the library and Horn Tech Center.

Laboratory, performing-arts and physical-education courses will continue to meet in person at this time.

"Students: please look for communications from instructors about plans for individual courses," Conoley said. "Reach out to your instructors if you have questions."

Normal instruction is expected to resume Monday, April 20.

"This action, I know, will cause great hardship," Conoley said. "It is, however, the appropriate action for our community to take."

The Daily Forty-Niner will continue to provide updated coverage as the story develops.

COVID prompted a campus shutdown, moving classes online in March 2020. Masks and muted interaction became the norm when in-person classes slowly started up again.

Parents and students on dorm move-in day, 2021.

Elise Noriega

Elise Noriega was a freshman psychology major when campus shut down in spring 2020.

"

At first I was excited because it was supposed to be a long Spring Break, which at that point, was much needed. When it was announced that we wouldn't be going back to campus for a while, I didn't know how to feel. I think a part of me was excited about it because I got to sleep in, but the other part of me was nervous about online schooling . . . The rest of that semester . . . happened. I think it was a big change for both students and professors, so the rest of that semester was kind of an adjustment period.

The next fall semester is when I really started to thrive online: I dually enrolled at CSULB and at LBCC so I could stay on top of classes, consistently talked to my academic advisor Vanessa (which helped so much when choosing my class schedule) and joined two clubs: Psychology Student Association and ProjectOCEAN. Once I started to attend the Zoom meetings for both of these clubs is when I began to feel a sense of community. I think my least favorite part . . . was the group projects. Having to rely on people who I didn't know, have never seen other than through a screen, and having to hope that they do their work was nerve-racking. Also, I felt like the social aspect of college was taken from me. During the three and a half years that it took me to get my degree, I was on campus for two full semesters and a few weeks in Spring 2020. I didn't have the opportunity to join a sorority, attend any of the Welcome Week activities like Smorgasport, and couldn't work in any of the research labs like I had wanted to.

Although there were parts of online school that I didn't like, I ended up really enjoying "Zoom University." I thrived because I got to do a lot of the work at my own pace, I could do school from anywhere, and I got to knock out a lot of classes during the winter and summer semesters, which ultimately led to me graduating early.

ANNA NGAI

Young Anna Ngai wasn't quite making it as a bank teller in Hong Kong. Although she had a "prestige job," she sometimes gave customers the wrong change, and the experience was stressing her out. During one of her breaks, a coworker said she should consider "seeing the world." The refugee from China thought that sounded like a good idea.

Always a curious, adventurous person, Ngai decided to pursue education at an American university. She applied to hundreds, and Cal State Long Beach was the first to accept her. She cobbled together enough money for a plane flight and a semester's tuition.

Business student Anna Ngai by the McIntosh Humanities Building in the early 1970s.

She flew into San Francisco and figured she'd walk the rest of the way to Long Beach. Someone at the San Francisco airport helped her read her ticket, which showed she had another leg left on her flight.

"I was very naive," she said. "I thought the US was like Hong Kong . . . I flunked my geography."

When she finally arrived, in 1971, Ngai recalled a "beautiful" campus. "At the time, flowers were blooming . . . peach flowers . . . it was so beautiful coming from Hong Kong, with buildings crowded together. It was like paradise. The Long Beach houses had flowers in front. I was not used to that openness."

In those days, international students could have a host family. "We don't have it now, I don't know when it stopped, but it was very helpful for foreign students . . . we come from a totally different culture and the American family would show us American traditions like Christmas, Thanksgiving," . . . and relatively temperate Southern California weather. Ngai came in January and brought warm clothes with her. Her host family bought her dresses and sandals. "I really appreciated that."

She earned money wearing a kimono for her hostess job at a fancy Fashion Island restaurant. She also worked as a nanny for a family at the Long Beach Yacht Club.

She graduated in 1974 with a business degree and cofounded two banks in Northern California, and along with her husband helped create several restaurant franchises in Northern California and Oregon.

By the early 2000s, she hit something like a midlife crisis. "I was working very hard to build up the business, helping my husband build up the business. I was working so hard and saw making money is not fulfilling. Even though the business was successful, I was not happy." She came across a Chinese phrase about helping people. "You see another person happy, you will be happy," she thought. "Instead of putting my attention on making money I decided I would do something good."

(Opposite page) The 1950s-era Soroptimist House, donated by Long Beach Soroptimists, was demolished to make way for the new alumni center.

She was thinking of creating a scholarship for her alma mater, but CSULB officials suggested donating to create an alumni center, something the campus was lacking despite the fact that it had more than 300,000 alums. School officials wanted to name the building after her, but she resisted.

"I at first didn't want to have my name on it . . . The school said yes, to use the name. I thought it was too showy. I was kind of embarrassed to have my name on it. I think some good deeds should not be boasted about. Kathy Kim, she worked for Long Beach State in those days and said I should put my name on for three reasons. One, I'm a woman. Two, I'm a minority. Three, I was a foreign student. As a foreign student, we can also give back to school, to our country. She thought I should have the name out there."

The $11.5 million, 5,500-square-foot Anna W. Ngai Alumni Center opened in 2022.

Ngai is retired from her businesses and now runs a foundation. "I have a comfortable life and I don't need a lot of stuff. Glad I'm able to use money to help the less privileged people. I like to see different countries, different people. That's the goal of my life now.

"The Chinese have a saying: A frog who lives in a well looks up at the sky and thinks the sky is as big as the well. When I get out I see the world is so big. All this starts with Cal State Long Beach."

President Jane Close Conoley and Anna Ngai open the Anna W. Ngai Alumni Center in 2022.

Class of 2021 grads who made it through the pandemic celebrate in the Brotman Hall fountain.

Lower campus was the scene for the main 2019 graduation ceremony.

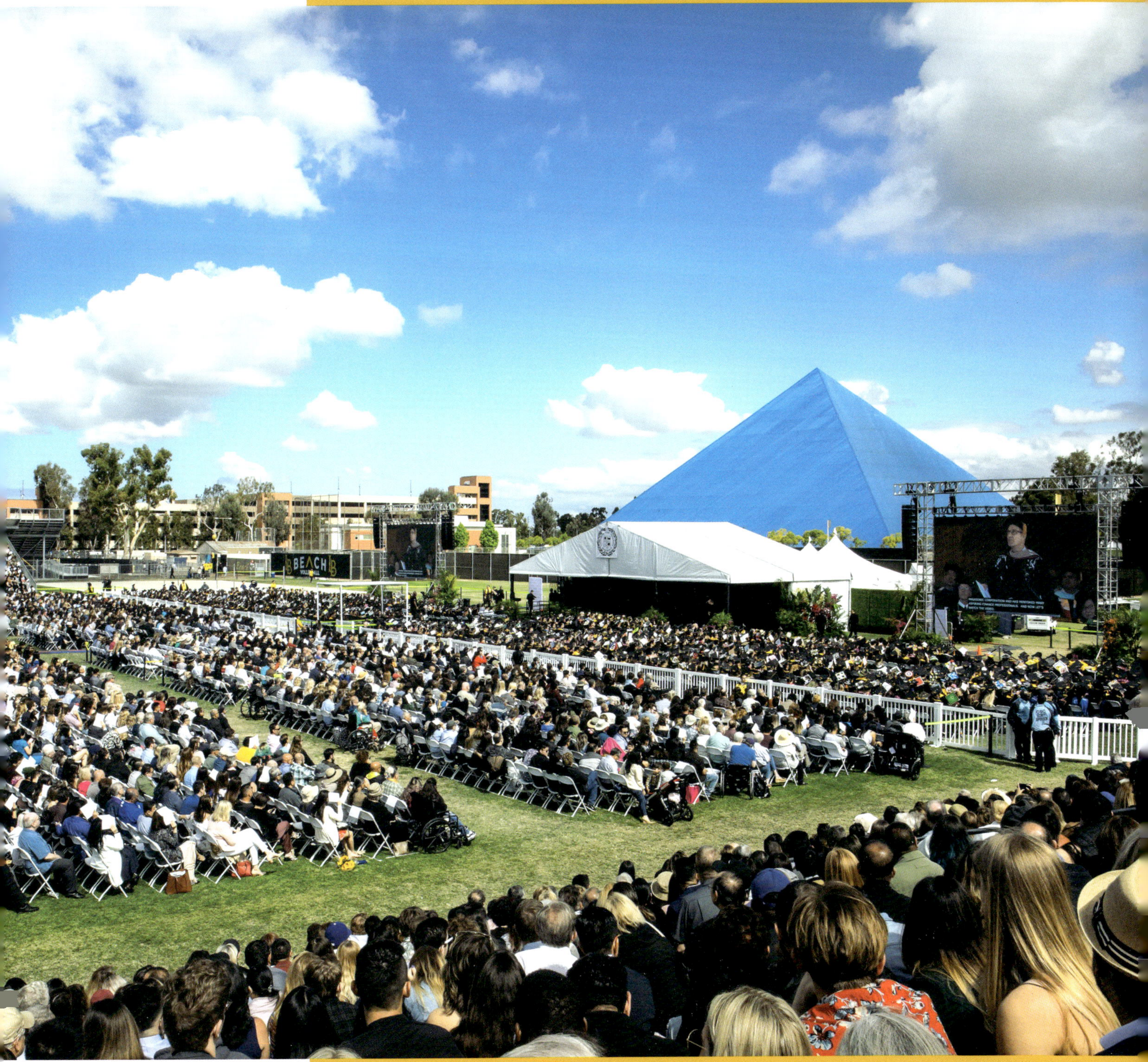
BEACH

2023!
RATULATIONS CLASS OF 2023!
CON
OF 202
Bally SPORTS

RATULATIONS CLASS OF 2023!
CONGRATULATIONS CLASS OF 2023!
StateFarm
TOYOTA
CSULB

The graduations continued at Angel Stadium through 2024. After a student outcry and petition campaign, student names were read and graduates walked the stage for the 2024 ceremony.

INDEX

PHOTO CREDITS

Photos are from the Long Beach State University Archives unless otherwise indicated:

Photo of Professor Irving Ahlquist, *Long Beach Press-Telegram*

Early 1950s aerial view of campus, Historical Society of Long Beach

Los Altos promotional pamphlet, Historical Society of Long Beach

Lloyd Whaley photo with President P. Victor Peterson, *Long Beach Press-Telegram*

First class photo, courtesy of Beverly O'Neill

John McConnell photos, courtesy of John McConnell

1959 photo of Lee Brown, courtesy Lee Brown

John McEuen photos, courtesy John McEuen

Jefferson Airplane photos, *Prospector* yearbook

1978 Craig Stone PowWow photos, courtesy Craig Stone

Anna NietoGomez photo, *Daily Forty-Niner*

1980 Tim Grobaty newsroom photo, courtesy of Tim Grobaty

Jerry Tarkanian with LBSU players photo, LBSU athletics

1973 plaque photo courtesy of Armando Vazquez-Ramos

Penny Toler photo, Long Beach State athletics

1989 women's volleyball team, LBSU athletics

Joan Bonvicini LaTaunya Pollard, *Daily Forty-Niner*

Professor Maulana Karenga, courtesy Maulana Karenga

1980s campus photo, Strategic Communications and University Research and Development

Dirtbags coach Dave Snow in dugout, LBSU athletics

Men's basketball coach Hank Greenberg photos, LBSU athletics

1994 photo of first President's Scholar class (later President's Scholarships), President's Scholars

Long Beach State football ends, *Long Beach Press-Telegram*

Professor Chris Lowe as a graduate student, courtesy of Chris Lowe

1994 Long Beach Walter Pyramid under construction, LBSU athletics

1993 women's volleyball champs, LBSU athletics

Misty May photos, LBSU athletics

Don Nelson photo courtesy of Chris Lowe

"CSULB to freeze admissions," *Daily Forty-Niner*

2006 Immigrant rights protest photos, Tracey J. Roman

Robert Maxson, F. King Alexander shaking hands, Tracey J. Roman

2018 men's volleyball championship players and crowd reaction, Trang Le, LBSU athletics

2018 Champs cover, *Daily Forty-Niner*

2020 Canceled cover, *Daily Forty-Niner*

Rashida Crutchfield photo, courtesy Rashida Crutchfield

2021 Pyramid workers, Barbara Kingsley-Wilson

Jane Close Conoley at 2023 convocation, Sean DuFrene, Strategic Communications, Dormitory move-in day photos, Sean DuFrene, Strategic Communications/ University Research and Development

2023 commencement Jane Close Conoley, Sean DuFrene, Strategic Communications

Graduation celebration photos from 2023, Sean DuFrene, Strategic Communications

2020 Puvungna photos, Richard H. Grant

"Para mi familia" photo, Richard. H. Grant

Graduation silhouette photo, Richard H. Grant

"She believed she could . . ." photo, Richard H. Gran

Student Recreation and Wellness Center construction and grand opening photos, ASI Communications

Student Success Center, Mary Zendejas photo, Strategic Communications

2021 graduates celebrating in Brotman Hall Fountain, Richard H. Grant

Drone photos of campus, William Liang

GO BEACH letters photo, Richard. H. Grant

Kleefeld Museum exterior, Tom Bonner

Anna Ngai photos, courtesy Anna Ngai and Strategic Communications

SOURCE LIST

1940s and 1950s

- Irving Ahlquist, interviewed by Sherna Berger Gluck, December 13, 1977, CSULB library archives.
- Isabel Patterson, interview by Cindy Cleary, February 7, 1979, CSULB library archives.
- Beverly O'Neill, interview with the author, May 25, 2014.
- P. Victor Peterson, former assemblyman William Grant and Don Gill of the CSULB Foundation, interviewed by Stephen Horn, February 25, 1971, transcript provided by the Peterson family.
- Memorandum from University Library Director Charles Boorkman, December 3. 1973, CSULB library archives.
- Ellie Johnson, interview with the author, May 1, 2014
- P. Victor Peterson, handwritten notes on the college founding, provided by the Peterson family.
- Interview with Francis "Frenchy" Flynn by Gene Asher, August 11, 1978, CSULB library archives.
- Remarks by Irving Ahlquist on August 27, 1999, at the College of Liberal Arts fiftieth anniversary luncheon.
- Daily Forty-Niner 35th Anniversary Issue, December 6, 1984.
- Interview with John McConnell March 31, 2022.
- Interview with Isabel Patterson conducted by Anthony Brennan, April 1987.
- Interview with Lee Brown, August 3, 2023.
- Richard Wilde, interviewed by Kaye Briegel, November 21, 1980, CSULB Digital Repository Library.

1960s

- Interview with Gary Little, March 24, 2022.
- Interview with Roman Kochan, November 8, 2022.
- Interview with Jonathan Talberg, September 17, 2023.
- Interview with Armando Vazquez-Ramos, May 10, 2023.
- Interview with Laura (Murphy) Terry, April 14, 2022.
- Interview with Rosemary Taylor Schmidt, January 20, 2015.
- Interview with Mwalimu (Donna) Evans, March 15, 2022.
- Interview with Anna NietoGomez, August 29, 2023.

1970s

- Interview with Craig Stone, November 30, 2022; December 14. 2023.
- Interview with Lawrence Fortenberry, February 18, 2022.
- Interview with Tim Grobaty, February 24, 2023.
- Interview with Jon Regnier, August, October 2014; March 14 and November 3, 2023.
- Information on Killingsworth, Brady and Smith, the Los Angeles Conservancy.
- Information provided by Roy Nakano, July 22, 2023.
- Information and interview with Glenn McDonald, September 15, 2014.
- Interview with Dee Abrahamse, August 4, 2014.
- Interview with David Bernstein, August 29, 2014.
- Stephen Horn interview with Ann Andriesse, August 7, 1991.
- Interview with Mark Mayuga, October 18, 2014.
- Interview with Joan Bonvicini, September 5, 2014.
- Interview with Dorothy Deatherage by Kaye Briegel, February 25, 1981, CSULB library archives.
- Pat Reid, interviewer unknown, November 19, 1979.
- Interview with Penny Toler, September 8, 2014.
- Interview with Isabel Patterson conducted by Anthony Brennan, April 1987.
- *African Americans in Long Beach and Southern California: A History*, by Claudine Burnett

1980s

- Interview with Julie Bartolotto, August 3, 2023.
- "An Early History of Women's Studies at California State University, Long Beach: 1968-1976" by Juliane Bartolotto.
- Interview with Dee Abrahamse, August 4, 2014.
- Interview with Seth Greenberg, May 25, 2022.
- Interview with Dave Snow, December 2014.

1990s

- Reviving Puvungna, An Archeological Project at Rancho Los Alamitos, by Keith Dixon, 1972.
- Interview with Maulana Karenga, November 4, 2023.
- Interview with Robert Maxson, July 31, 2014.
- Interview with Valerie Bordeaux, August 12. 2014.
- Interview with Doug Robinson, August 21, 2014.
- Interview with Stu Rosen, December 2014.
- Interview with Craig Stone, November 30, 2022; December 14. 2023.
- Interview with Cindi Alvitre, March 26 and 28, 2015.
- Interview with Danielle Scott, August 7, 2023.
- Interview with Brian Gimmillaro, July 18, 2014, August 9, 2023.
- Interview with Misty May, August 15, 2014.
- Interview with Melissa Ohta, November 29, 2014.
- Interview with Scott Charmack, January 4, 2015; June 26, 2023.
- Interview with Dianne Asis, December 21, 2014.
- Interview with Robert Garcia, February 20, 2023.

2000s

- Interview with F. King Alexander, April 7, 2022; January 20, 2024.
- Interview with Chris Lowe, June 16, 2023.
- Information provided by Austin Lewis, December 1, 2023.
- Interview with Alan Knipe, June 21, 2022.
- Interview with Nick Amado, August 14, 2023.
- Information on the Shakarian Family Student Success Center and Bob Murphy Access Center from CSULB Strategic Communications.
- Interview with Rashida Crutchfield, March 20, 2023.
- Interview with Paul Baker Prindle, Aug. 30, 2023.
- Information provided by Alexa Abudayyeh, November 30, 2023.
- Information provided by Elise Noriega, November 26, 2023.
- Information provided by Rachel Barnes, November 27, 2023.
- Interview with Jane Close Conoley, January 26, 2024.
- Interview with Anna Ngai, May 31, 2023.